T0324563

A Good and Dignified Life

JOKE J. HERMSEN

A Good and Dignified Life

THE POLITICAL ADVICE OF HANNAH ARENDT AND ROSA LUXEMBURG

*Translated from the Dutch by
Brendan Monaghan*

A MARGELLOS
WORLD REPUBLIC OF LETTERS BOOK

Yale UNIVERSITY PRESS | NEW HAVEN & LONDON

N ederlands
letterenfonds
dutch foundation
for literature

This publication has been made possible with financial support from the Dutch Foundation for Literature.

The Margellos World Republic of Letters is dedicated to making literary works from around the globe available in English through translation. It brings to the English-speaking world the work of leading poets, novelists, essayists, philosophers, and playwrights from Europe, Latin America, Africa, Asia, and the Middle East to stimulate international discourse and creative exchange.

Yale University Press books may be purchased in quantity for educational, business, or promotional use. For information, please email sales.press@yale.edu (U.S. office) or sales@yaleup.co.uk (U.K. office).

Set in Source Serif type by Motto Publishing Services, Austin, Texas.
Printed in the United States of America.

Library of Congress Control Number: 2021949551
ISBN 978-0-300-25925-4 (hardcover : alk. paper)

A catalogue record for this book is available from the British Library.

This paper meets the requirements of ANSI/NISO Z39.48-1992 (Permanence of Paper).

10 9 8 7 6 5 4 3 2 1

Contents

A Good and Dignified Life

1

When I started reading Rosa Luxemburg's writings in late summer 2018, political protests had already flared up around our village in Burgundy. People were up in arms against President Emmanuel Macron because, despite election promises, he hadn't done anything for the impoverished French countryside and wanted to increase fuel taxes. Whether they had a job or not, few people were getting by, while the elite was treated to tax breaks, with the scrapping of the wealth tax. The election promises of Macron's En Marche! party had proven to be hollow; life had only become more expensive and difficult. 'On n'en peut plus'—we can't take it anymore—my neighbor complained; having worked as a nurse for many years, she struggled on a very modest pension. Within a few weeks, it became clear that this personal lament reflected a far more widespread sense of frustration, which soon grew into a protracted popular uprising, not only in Burgundy but throughout France.

Most people in the Nièvre—the western part of Burgundy, where we have been restoring an old inn for the past ten years—once worked in agriculture or forestry or ran a village café, bakery, or grocery store, as my neighbor's mother had done all her life. But most of the cafés and shops in the villages in our area have now closed, and a handful of farmers cultivate the many thousands of acres of agricultural land. For groceries, people must drive to one of the large supermarkets, which pay farmers less and less for their grain and milk. Visiting a doctor, post office, or pharmacy also involves traveling many kilometers by car. That's why the government's proposed fuel price hike went down so badly and had such a dramatic fallout a little later.

Writers like Victor Hugo and Emile Zola described the poverty and difficult living conditions of the lower classes in French society in nineteenth-century novels, for example, *Les Misérables* (1862) and *Germinal* (1885). More than a century later, economic inequality and class differences are again the subject of writers, among them Annie Ernaux, Didier Eribon, and Édouard Louis. With barely concealed rage, Louis—son of a worker disabled in a factory accident—denounces French political leaders in *Who Killed My Father* (2018), reproaching them for social dominance and contempt for the lower classes. In October 2018, the young writer delivered an inspired reading about his book to a sold-out Paradiso, the Amsterdam music venue that has hosted pop giants like the Rolling Stones, Patti Smith, Pink Floyd, Prince, Amy Winehouse, and David Bowie. He argued that neoliberal capitalism, combined with elitism and technocracy, has created an underclass in France, condemned to a 'miserable' and inhumane existence. He predicted this would lead to great political unrest and was proven right sooner than even he could have expected. Just two weeks later, the first protesters, donning yellow vests, occupied roads and roundabouts and organized demonstrations against Macron's policy in large and smaller French cities for more than seventy (!) Saturdays in a row.

France was not the only scene of political protests in 2018.

In other European countries, such as Spain, Italy, Serbia, Austria, Poland, and Germany, people also took to the streets in large numbers that year, protesting economic injustice, sexual violence, or, under the surprising leadership of Swedish schoolgirl Greta Thunberg, the climate crisis. Even in my own country, the Netherlands—more famous for its 'polder model,' the Dutch policy of compromise, than its revolutionary élan—2018 heralded the start of an impressive series of demonstrations against cutbacks in health care and education—with professors marching side by side with students for the first time in history—the racist 'Black Pete' folklore, and the climate crisis.

Not only did temperatures rise and glaciers melt, but emotions also grew more heated across the world, as the political climate wasn't all that different outside Europe. After the 'Arab Spring,' which set off a wave of uprisings and revolutions in Tunisia, Egypt, Libya, Syria, Iran, and Yemen, starting in December 2010, people in India, Brazil, Venezuela, Chile, the United States, and Hong Kong also took to the streets in great numbers over the ensuing years to demonstrate against poverty, violence, political oppression, or political leaders' corruption. Record numbers of demonstrators participated in many places. Protest marches in the United States, including the Women's March against discrimination and sexual violence, and the March for Our Lives in support of gun control legislation, drew between one and a half and two million people. The murder of the unarmed, twenty-two-year-old African American Stephon Clark by Sacramento police sparked a series of demonstrations against police brutality. With the murder of George Floyd less than two years later, this developed into the global protest movement Black Lives Matter.

The Black Lives Matter demonstrations have strongly influenced the debate on racism and police brutality in the United States, and elsewhere too. Despite the coronavirus pandemic, many hundreds of thousands of demonstrators joined protests against racism in European cities in spring 2020. As in America, French demonstrations were often about police violence; in the United Kingdom they focused on racism in the Commonwealth, and in Germany and the Netherlands on institutional racism. More than fifty years after Martin Luther King Jr.'s historic speech at the March on Washington in 1963, the awareness that racism must be actively combated finally seems to be turning into actual policy by regional and national governments.

Social media were pivotal in spreading the flames of protest, as was the case in the Arab Spring and the climate demonstrations. The shocking images of the murder of George Floyd and calls to take part in public protests appeared almost instantaneously on people's mobile telephones. Individual anger or outrage at police brutality could be translated directly into collective action. Social media have developed into an important instrument for political mobilization in the past decade. The Black Lives Matter slogans and hashtags have also inspired other liberation movements. Demonstrations in May 2021 against Israel's occupation of Palestinian territories often included banners like 'Palestinians can't breathe' and 'Palestinian Lives Matter.' Especially younger generations are uniting across the world on social media, revolting against oppression, dispossession, and discrimination.

Mass protests by the yellow vests in France, which I saw with my own eyes from autumn 2018, also mainly organized on social media. This revolt didn't come out of the blue; the ground had been prepared by various other protests in the preceding years. Only in autumn 2018 did it become clear that the French population was prepared to use what French philosophers such as Simone Weil and Albert Camus considered one of the most essential characteristics of the human condition, that is, their *pouvoir du refus*, their ability to refuse and say no. The opening sentences of Albert Camus's work *The Rebel* read as follows: 'What is a rebel? A man who says no, but whose refusal does not imply a renunciation. He is also a man who says yes, from the moment he makes his first gesture of rebellion.' Camus's rebel only really knows one thing for sure: it is impossible to continue down this same path. For Camus, 'no' means drawing a clear line in the sand. Our ability to say no refers to the possibility of intervening in the course of things, and from this intervention—which assumes a temporary suspension—giving birth to something new. The 'no' can only develop into a new 'yes' after a boundary has been indicated. The rebel 'is acting in the name of certain values which are still indeterminate,' Camus writes, 'but which he feels are common to himself and to all men.'

There has been a widely shared sense that things must change in recent years. Alongside the United States and France, this is very clear in the United Kingdom, where Europe was rejected wholesale when a slim majority (51.9 percent) of Britons said no to membership of the European Union in a referendum. I clearly remember how, after celebrating my daughter's twenty-fourth birthday on the night of June 23–24, 2016, we woke to the news that seventeen million people in Britain had voted for Brexit. Even though we had seen it coming, we could hardly believe our ears. It felt like a shockwave had reverberated through the old continent. The United Kingdom had ditched Europe, shaking its very foundations for an instant.

Pro-Brexit demonstrators didn't wear yellow vests, but they did share the same dissatisfaction in and distrust of both national and European politics as their French confrères two years later. They often came from regions with similar socioeconomic characteristics, suffering high levels of poverty and unemployment, government retrenchment, and an exodus of the young. They felt they were the losers in a globalized world which favored large metropolitan areas. Extreme right-wing parties like Nigel Farage's UKIP also fueled their fear of mass immigration. 'Take back control' became the infamous slogan of the Brexit campaign. But as in France, the real prelude to the Brexit vote was the global financial crisis of 2008 and the ensuing global recession.

Britain's Conservative government seized upon the global financial crisis to introduce sweeping austerity. It lowered incomes, scrapped social security benefits, and capped civil servants' pay rises below inflation. This 'age of austerity,' as Prime Minister David Cameron called it, was of course largely shouldered by those least able to shoulder it and by the most vulnerable regions. While the banking industry was rescued, many Britons were reduced to living at or below the poverty line. As in rural France, local and regional governments were forced to slash public services: post offices, libraries, and schools were closed. Future perspectives became more and more limited and meager—until a substantial part of the British population couldn't stomach austerity any longer. Rising in revolt, they said 'leave' to Europe, mistakenly holding it responsible for their deprivation. It wasn't so much Europe as the international banking crisis that was to blame for their hopelessness.

A popular uprising always happens unexpectedly, I learned that October 2018 from Rosa Luxemburg (1871–

1919) and the French *gilets jaunes* (yellow vests). Mass protests are seldom directed from above, usually arising from below, among the population; the moment the revolt is sparked is therefore unsure. There's something intangible and uncertain at the heart of every political struggle, Luxemburg argued in *The Mass Strike, the Political Party and the Trade Unions* in 1906, because political revolts don't follow 'ready-made formulae' or party doctrines but depend on the will of the people, who can be very fickle and capricious as history has shown. Although uncertainty makes it difficult to organize uprisings, we should still appreciate their value because they guarantee our freedom of thought and action, Luxemburg wrote in her explicitly critical text *The Russian Revolution* in 1918. In this discourse, she accused Lenin of almost immediately replacing this freedom with dogmatic rules and unconditional loyalty to the party in an attempt to eliminate as much uncertainty as possible.

More than a century ago, Rosa Luxemburg advocated socioeconomic justice in the world, which she believed could only be achieved when the dictatorial rule of the Russian tsar and the German kaiser had been replaced by socialist democracy. Both monarchs had been toppled by the end of 1918, but it didn't lead, in either Russia or Germany, to the democracy, partly based on citizen councils, she had envisioned. Luxemburg was extremely critical of both Russian revolutionary and German social democratic rule up to her death. For her, criticism, resistance, and revolt were preeminent political acts, expressing the uniquely human ability to say 'no' to injustice and 'yes' to 'unlimited' democracy: 'The only way to a rebirth is the school of public life itself, the most unlimited, the broadest democracy and public opinion.'

Rosa Luxemburg was driven by a strong desire for social justice and political freedom, even though it landed her in prison time and again. Independent thinking, autonomous judgment, and freedom of speech were infinitely more important to her than toeing the party line. 'Self-criticism, remorseless, cruel, and going to the core of things is the life's breath and light of the proletarian movement,' she wrote in *The Crisis of Social Democracy*. In her eyes, Lenin practiced dictatorial power politics in 1917, granted Bolsheviks improper privileges, and wanted to deprive people of all political freedom. 'Clearly not uncritical apologetics but thoughtful criticism is alone capable of bringing out the treasures of experiences and teachings,' she wrote in her critical account, *The Russian Revolution*, in 1917. For Rosa Luxemburg, democratic socialism hadn't been achieved in Russia 'but lies completely hidden in the mists of the future.' Lenin was furious, ordering the burning of all copies of the book. Fortunately for us, and our ability to interpret history truthfully, he was unsuccessful.

It was Hannah Arendt (1906–1973) who led me to Luxemburg's work that late summer 2018 in the French countryside, when I was rereading her essay *Men in Dark Times* (1968). 'How much reality must be retained even in a world become inhuman if humanity is not to be reduced to an empty phrase or a phantom?' Arendt asked, and she sought answers in the works of such writers as Karl Jaspers, Bertolt Brecht, Walter Benjamin, and Rosa Luxemburg. The world grows dark when people no longer feel collective responsibility, only concern themselves with their individual interests, and distrust the political sphere such that they turn their backs on it. Arendt also calls this danger of depoliticization—'worldlessness'—which 'is always a form of barbarism' in her view.

I had already read *Men in Dark Times*—having studied Hannah Arendt's work since the 1980s—but a few weeks later I returned to it with renewed interest and a certain sense of urgency, partly thanks to the gilets jaunes. The key question in this book is the extent to which we are currently in danger of ending up in 'dark times' again. The French revolt, but also America's presidential elections, have exposed the issue once more as uncomfortably topical, with nationalism and xenophobia reemerging everywhere, capitalism still reigning supreme, and trust in political institutions diminishing.

In late 2016 American professor of political science Jeffrey C. Isaac asked, in the *Washington Post,* how Hannah Arendt's 1951 book *The Origins of Totalitarianism* 'could . . . speak so powerfully to our present moment.' Various political commentators turned to this masterpiece on dictatorial and totalitarian regimes, with which Arendt made her name as a political thinker some seventy years ago. A passage in the preface, which seemed to articulate many Americans' trepidation, was particularly often quoted: 'This moment of anticipation is like the calm that settles after all hopes have died. We no longer hope for an eventual restoration of the old world order with all its traditions, or for the reintegration of the masses of five continents who have been thrown into a chaos produced by the violence of wars and revolutions and the growing decay of all that has still been spared. Under the most diverse conditions and disparate circumstances, we watch the development of the same phenomena—homelessness on an unprecedented scale, rootlessness to an unprecedented depth. Never has our future been more unpredictable, never have we depended so much on political forces that cannot be trusted to follow the rules of common sense and self-interest—forces that look like sheer insanity, if judged by the standards of other centuries.'

Hannah Arendt wrote this book on the rise and func-
tioning of totalitarian regimes because she wanted and 'had
to understand' how the 'unimaginable' terror in Nazi Germany could have occurred and because she argued we must
be vigilant for the reemergence of tyranny, despotism, and
demagoguery even after the war. Arendt was in a unique position to understand her subject matter: born to Jewish par-
ents in Hannover in 1906, she fled the Nazis in the 1930s and
finally settled in New York. Recent years have seen a marked
increase in interest in her work. One of the reasons for this
is because Arendt connected her philosophical reflections
on humankind with incisive analyses that often contained a
warning to democratic societies. While in many respects the
world has changed significantly since the 1950s, her warn-
ings have unfortunately lost precious little of their urgency.

To Arendt, totalitarianism was a political system dominated by power, instrumentality, and technocracy, with no
place for freedom, humanity, and solidarity. Totalitarian
systems are almost always based on absolute faith in a single idea or a single people, and so they mostly have a scapegoat theory, like anti-Semitism in Nazi Germany. There is no
space for open debate or divergent interpretations and opinions in this kind of system because everything is coerced in
the logic of a single people or idea. Totalitarian regimes aim
to turn a heterogeneous people into a uniform and docile
mass. Their principal aim isn't to change society, as they
ceaselessly claim, but rather human nature. They want to
transform it by destroying everything Arendt considers essential to it—natality, plurality, spontaneity, and freedom—
in the service of their one ideology.

The National Socialists deployed fear, propaganda, and
terror as the principal weapons with which to achieve this

transformation. Over time, large sections of the German population no longer dared to think critically, or they lost their ability to do so, gave up resisting, and no longer independently formed their opinions. Arendt argues that the evil that civilians subsequently perpetrated in imitation of their political leaders didn't so much stem from the depths of their souls as from fear and a lack of political consciousness and critical thinking. The greatest threats to democracy are a cowed and subdued people, rendered indifferent, and giving preference to a specific group or race. Toward the end of her voluminous analysis, Arendt warns that totalitarianism is a 'form of government which as a potentiality and an ever-present danger is only too likely to stay with us from now on.' Freedom is a fragile achievement which we must continuously fight for. When demagogues raise their voices then it is time to exercise vigilance and safeguard democratic gains.

In her essay on Rosa Luxemburg, Arendt makes no secret of her admiration for the Polish-Jewish writer and politician, who became an icon for the fight against injustice over the course of the twentieth century. Arendt's praise surprised me at first because I'd thought that her criticism of Marxism would have ruled out much sympathy with Luxemburg's ideas, but I was wrong. She even called Luxemburg's study *The Accumulation of Capital* (1913) 'a work of genius' and praised her desire for political freedom and her call for nonviolent resistance. Toward the end of her essay, Arendt wonders whether 'history [will] look different if seen through the prism of her life and work.'

I was intrigued and started reading Luxemburg's work, while the protests around us in Burgundy grew louder and the first placards demanding the Macron's resignation were plastered on walls and bus shelters. I'd never read any of Luxemburg's writings, perhaps a bit put off by the cult associated with her. Yet to my surprise, I discovered in them common ground with my own work, not only thoughts on the increasing pressure of work in a society where time has become 'money,' and the alienation, despair, and stress this causes, but also concepts such as spontaneity, political freedom, and the popular or citizens' councils, which play an important role in Hannah Arendt's work.

Rosa Luxemburg, born and raised in a Jewish family in Poland at the end of the nineteenth century, was convinced that a popular uprising could succeed only if it arose 'spontaneously' from the people. Spontaneity represented for her, as for Arendt, the freedom people can take to initiate something new, which can bring about a necessary interruption or revolution in the old system. The conditions for this kind of spontaneous interventions are critical consciousness, political commitment to the world, and enthusiasm; the means available to people are demonstrations and strikes, and also organizing lectures and debates, writing newspaper articles, essays, and pamphlets, and—as importantly—critical voices joining forces in clubs, movements, or associations, after which joint political action can be taken.

Striking, taking to the streets, making one's voice heard, and political organization were, to Luxemburg, the most effective way of bringing about change. She particularly wanted to make the working class conscious of their capacity for political action, traveling all over Europe in the early twentieth century to make them 'suddenly and sharply . . . realize how intolerable was that social and economic existence which they had patiently endured for decades in the chains of capitalism,' as she wrote in *The Mass Strike* (1906). Luxemburg was also a political thinker with a strong pedagogic and emancipatory agenda; she insisted everyone should have equal access to good education and taught for years at the central school of the Social Democratic Party of Germany (SPD), where she was an immensely popular lecturer. Good education was in her view essential to critical thinking. She often repeated Ferdinand Lassalle's phrase 'The most revolutionary act is and forever remains to say loudly what is.' Acquiring knowledge is indispensable for developing a clear view of the world 'as it really is' and subsequently for initiating spontaneous action. The converse is, surprisingly, also true. As Luxemburg put it in one of the famous statements credited to her: 'Those who do not move do not notice their chains.'

On her European tour, Rosa Luxemburg visited Poland, Russia, Switzerland, and the Netherlands. Dutch support for democratic socialism had grown considerably since the railroad strike of 1903; she befriended Dutch luminaries, including poet and writer Henriette Roland Holst, Socialist politician Pieter Jelles Troelstra, and poet Herman Gorter. She addressed a packed audience in the Concertgebouw in Amsterdam in 1904, proclaiming the need for economic justice and international solidarity, which was often undermined by disputes. 'Whoever saw Rosa Luxemburg in Amsterdam those days,' Henriette Roland Holst wrote in her biography on Luxemburg in 1935, 'as she walked through the sunny streets, swaying her hips, her face blossoming with relief after the exertion of hours of speaking, her voice and smile filled with charm and exuberance—whoever saw her like that retained the memory of an extraordinarily charming creature.' Her letters and biographies by Nettl (1966), Frohlich (1967), and Hetmann (1976) reveal a politician committed to humanity, an astute intellectual who sometimes silenced her political opponents with caustic ridicule, and a passionate activist who considered it her lifelong task to fight injustice and poverty in the world.

2

The first work I read that summer by Rosa Luxemburg was her letters, which immediately won me over. As well as her invigorating style, she revealed a deep love of literature, music, and art—with Goethe, Mozart, and Rembrandt her favorites—and she tirelessly expressed what Hannah Arendt would later call *amor mundi*: love and responsibility for the world. 'I feel at home in the entire world, wherever there are clouds and birds and human tears,' she wrote in a letter from prison in February 1917. She actually had little more than a few 'amazingly beautiful pink clouds above the walls of my fortress' or a great tit singing outside her barred window. Her world had been reduced to a dark cell, where she tried to feel at home with a few plant cuttings and books.

That is where she wrote her famous *Letters from Prison*, first published in German in 1920 and in English in 1923, which languished for half a century before republication, and now is available to new readers all over the world thanks to many new translations. Verso published an extensive new translation, *The Letters of Rosa Luxemburg* in 2011, containing 250 letters, which was well received by critics; it is some of the most beautiful correspondence from the early twentieth century. She wrote the following to her friend Sophie Liebknecht in May 1917.

There was a thunderstorm [yesterday evening]. I shall never forget what followed. . . . A pale, dull, spectral twilight suddenly diffused itself over the landscape, so that it seemed as if the whole prospect were under a thick grey veil. A gentle rain was falling steadily upon the leaves; sheet lightning flamed at brief intervals, tinting the leaden grey with flashes of purple, while the distant thunder could still be heard rumbling like the declining waves of a heavy sea. Then, quite abruptly, the nightingale began to sing in the sycamore in front of my window. Despite the rain, the lightning and the thunder, the notes rang out as clear as a bell. The bird sang as if intoxicated, as if possessed, as if wishing to drown the thunder, to illuminate the twilight. Never have I heard anything so lovely. On the background of the alternately leaden and lurid sky, the song seemed to show like shafts of silver. It was so mysterious, so incredibly beautiful, that involuntarily I murmured the last verse of Goethe's poem, 'Oh, wert thou here!'

Luxemburg's letters have a completely different style than her political texts, which have a more combative tone, I would say, and were partly written in the Marxist idiom common at the time, but which now comes across as a bit outdated and obsolete. Her letters, in contrast, sparkle with idiosyncrasy and originality. Hannah Arendt described them in her essay "A Heroine of Revolution" (1966) in the *New Yorker* as 'of a simple, touchingly humane, and often of poetic beauty.' I wholeheartedly agree; rarely have I read correspondence in which the writer's voice spoke to me so expressively and close at hand, as though she'd written the lines yesterday and not a century ago. What is more, the letters 'were enough to destroy the propaganda image of bloodthirsty "Red Rosa,"' as Arendt noted. In fact, she was the 'most anti-militarist' of all the revolutionaries of her time. Arendt's opinion was undoubtedly influenced by her husband Heinrich Blucher's personal anecdotes—he'd fought as a student alongside Luxemburg and Liebknecht in the Spartacist uprising in Berlin in 1918.

Besides acquiring knowledge about the world and nature, Luxemburg considered being *ein guter Mensch*, a good human being—leading a good and dignified life—the most noble human pursuit and not a term of abuse, as is common among some skeptics today. 'See that you remain a human being,' she urged Mathilde Wurm. 'Being a human being is the main thing, above all else. And that means: to be firm and clear and cheerful, yes, cheerful, in spite of everything and anything.' I found the letters also remarkably 'cheerful,' especially given the unpleasant conditions in which they were written: for mocking the kaiser, Luxemburg was incarcerated in a cold prison cell, where she and many others were 'packed next to one another like sardines.'

Luxemburg was imprisoned in 1916 for over two years for her strong pacifist convictions and repeated calls 'not to take up arms against our brothers.' When her party, the Social Democratic Party of Germany, agreed in August 1914 to approve increased war credits in parliament and to support the kaiser's war against France, Luxemburg was devastated. She could never understand why her fellow party members didn't see that this would lead to a devastating war, mainly affecting its own supporters. From prison, she continued fiercely opposing the war, which was conducted chiefly for economic and 'imperialist' interests in her opinion—sharing the spoils of colonized land. She wasn't released until autumn 1918, when the First World War came to an end, having claimed more than fifteen million lives, making it one of the most violent conflicts in history. Her days were numbered by then. Only a few months later, on January 15, 1919, Rosa Luxemburg was murdered in cold blood during the short-lived revolution that had broken out in postwar Germany.

Reading her letters in Burgundy that summer, I was struck not only by the perspicacity of her analysis and the poetic power of her words but also by their hopeful tone. Aside from occasional visitors, she'd only had her books, plant cuttings, and the few birds outside her barred window for company in those years. And yet she never lost heart, kept working and writing, and rarely gave up hope for better times. The long missives she sent her friends 'outside,' like bright flares shot across the prison's high fortress walls, tried to dispel their despair and dejection. 'Don't forget, as busy as you may be, as you're hurrying across the courtyard in pursuit of the day's pressing tasks, do not forget to quickly raise your head and cast a glance at those silver great clouds and that silent blue ocean in which they are swimming,' she wrote to a friend. 'Take notice of the resplendence and glory that overlies this day, because this day will never, ever come again! This day is a gift to you like a rose in full bloom, lying at your feet, waiting for you to pick it up and press it to your lips.'

Time and again she remarked that 'everything will come out right in the end' or things 'are about to develop into something colossal.' She not only tried to encourage her friends but also drew their attention to the beauty of nature, poetry, or art, which offered some shelter, so that they would still feel 'at home' in the world. She recommended countless books to her friends—much Goethe, Dostoevsky, Korolenko, and Anatole France—and music, like Gounod's *Ave Maria*, Mozart, or Hugo Wolf's songs.

In a letter dated November 1917, she wrote to Sophie, Karl Liebknecht's wife:

> You know, Sonitschka, that the longer it takes, and the more the baseness and atrocities occurring every day transgress all limits and bounds, the more calm and resolute I do become. Just as I cannot apply moral standards to the elements, to a hurricane, a flood, or a solar eclipse, and instead, consider them only something given, an object of research and knowledge. . . . I have a feeling that this whole moral mire through which we are now wading, this huge madhouse in which we are living, can overnight, with the wave of a magic wand, be transformed into its opposite, transformed into something extraordinarily great and heroic. . . . We must take everything that happens in society the same way as in private life: calmly, generously and with a mild smile. I firmly believe that, in the end, after the war, or at the close of the war, everything will turn out alright.

Where did she get the reserves of hope to write such letters, despite having been imprisoned for two years by then, and dedicate herself to articles and pamphlets, which were smuggled out of prison, agitating until the very last day for the end of the war? I must confess that these letters also profoundly changed my image of 'Red Rosa,' vainly driving people to the revolutionary barricades. From the very first time I read them, they transformed the image, cultivated by parties on both the left and right, of an unflinching politician into that of an intelligent, courageous woman, committed to humanity, who wrote on the most diverse subjects with an exceptionally astute mind and an even more incisive pen. From flowering mimosa to political and economic issues, from chirping sparrows and tits to Russian, Polish, and German literature, there was actually very little that Rosa Luxemburg wasn't interested in.

One of the most poignant examples is her Christmas letter to Sophie Liebknecht at the end of December 1917.

> This is my third Christmas in the clink, . . . but you should certainly not take that tragically. . . . I lie there quietly, alone, wrapped in these many-layered black veils of darkness, boredom, lack of freedom, and winter—and at the same time my heart is racing with an incomprehensible, unfamiliar inner joy as though I were walking across a flowering meadow in radiant sunshine. And in the dark I smile at life, as if I knew some sort of magical secret that gives the lie to everything evil and sad and changes it into pure light and happiness. . . . I believe that the secret is nothing other than life itself; the deep darkness of night is so beautiful and as soft as velvet, if one only looks at it the right way. . . . At such moments I think of you and I would like so much to pass on this magical key to you, so that always and in all situations you would be aware of the beautiful and the joyful. . . . I am certainly not thinking of foisting off on you some sort of asceticism or made-up joys. . . . I would only like to pass on to you my inexhaustible inner cheerfulness, so that I could be at peace about you and not worry, so that you could go through life wearing a cloak covered with stars, which would protect you against everything petty and trivial. . . . Sonyichka, dearest, in spite of everything be calm and cheerful. Life is like that, one must take it as it is, [and remain] brave, undaunted, and smiling—in spite of everything.

Her hope and these words of encouragement spoke to Hannah Arendt too. She concluded her essay on Rosa Luxemburg in the *New Yorker* (1966) with the following words: 'One would like to believe that there is still hope for a belated recognition of who she was and what she did, as one would like to hope that she will finally find her place in the education of political scientists.' It seems that this hope still resonates more than half a century later, given the many republications of Luxemburg's work and international conferences organized in Paris, Berlin, Madrid, Seoul, Amsterdam, and Chicago in recent years. Various new essays and studies on her work have also been published, among them Jacqueline Rose's fascinating book *Women in Dark Times* (2014), Jason Schulman's *Rosa Luxemburg: Her Life and Legacy* (2013), Diane Lamoureux' *Pensées rebelles* (Rebellious Thoughts, 2012), Simone Frieling's *Rebellinnen* (Rebels, 2018), Norman Geras's *The Legacy of Rosa Luxemburg* (2015), Dana Naomi Mill's interesting new biography *Critical Lives: Rosa Luxemburg* (2020), and Kate Evans' wonderful graphic novel *Red Rosa* (2018).

Besides her letters, there have recently been new translations of various other texts by Rosa Luxemburg, such as *The Russian Revolution* and *The Accumulation of Capital*, into English, Spanish, and Dutch. This is certainly hopeful. Of course, one could counter that hope blinds. Perhaps—but without hope, we can be certain nothing will ever change. Rosa Luxemburg was convinced that we had to change the course of history and could no longer continue down the same capitalist and imperialist path, for the sake of nature and humankind. As long as there is time to live, there is hope, as an old proverb goes. In these times of growing turmoil and uncertainty, we need hopeful perspectives to overcome fear and disappointment and to bear our sense of loss and transience. Without this hope, we cannot believe in the promise of new beginnings, or the possibility of change.

American writer and activist Rebecca Solnit argued in *Hope in the Dark* in 2004 that 'hope is a gift you don't have to surrender, a power you don't have to throw away.' It's certainly a power Rosa Luxemburg didn't lack; her letters show again and again how hope was one of the main drivers of her political struggle. But the question is how many people nowadays would still consider this motivating force self-evident. 'Your opponents would love you to believe that it's hopeless,' Solnit writes, 'that there's no reason to act, that you can't win.' Luxemburg had been convinced since childhood that capitalism was a destructive system, in both humanitarian and ecological terms, and that it must be transformed into another socioeconomic model, while many of us suppose no other system is possible. That won't do much good. How are we going to make progress like this? How can we tackle these problems if we only view the world with skepticism or cynicism?

Rebecca Solnit offers hope for change because she believes that, despite increasing inequality and the threat posed by the climate crisis, important reforms can also be observed. These include the growth of protest groups against sexual and ethnic violence, the spread of grassroots movements against current climate policy, and mounting criticism—even in economic circles—of hypercapitalism. In Solnit's view, hope doesn't mean turning a blind eye to injustice, but recognizing its consequences and seeing how things can be different and better. She isn't telling a story of how 'everything will get better' but is interested in hopeful narratives about prospects, with specific opportunities and possibilities beckoning on the horizon.

We must draw hope from the stories of others, Belgian-Albanian philosopher Bleri Lleshi argues in his book *De kracht van hoop* (The Power of Hope, 2018). Inspired by Martin Luther King Jr.'s life and work, Lleshi writes that 'in times of cynicism, we have come to see hope more and more as something naïve, while hope might actually be able to move us forward.' Listening carefully and closely observing our surroundings are the preconditions for discovering hopeful initiatives amid bad tidings, a quest that German-Jewish philosopher Ernst Bloch also calls 'the working of the principle of hope.' In his magnum opus on hope, the voluminous tome *The Principle of Hope* (published in 1955, translated into English in 1986), Bloch convincingly argues that feelings of hope and expectation can encourage people to no longer settle for the current world, ruled by destructive forces. He links political and philosophical analyses of hope to myths, sagas, music, art, and literature, demonstrating how human beings, despite their melancholic sense of time and transience, are fundamentally beings who hope and desire. Above all, this hope allows us to examine critically the status quo, go off the beaten track, and develop ourselves and society sustainably. 'It is a question of learning hope,' Bloch writes, as 'the emotion of hope . . . makes people broad instead of confining them.'

Hope isn't a woolly concept but a condition for resisting and no longer silently assenting to current policy. Hope is a counterpoint to melancholy; it safeguards us from excessive dejection or clinging too much to loss and parting, so we can focus on what has 'not yet' been achieved. These two small words, 'not yet,' are a fine distillation of the power of hope. We can hope for all that has *not yet* been thought, composed, or described. 'Time is hope,' Bloch asserts in one of the shortest definitions of time ever given. People aren't completed or realized constitutions—as, say, a table that can be 'finished'—their consciousness of time, their linguistic abilities, and their imagination make them face 'the substratum of real possibilities,' a horizon of the 'not yet.' This 'not yet' can be glimpsed with the right knowledge and attention; Bloch says art, music, and poetry can sharpen this intuition because they arise from the boundary between the possible and impossible, the sayable and ineffable, the certain and uncertain. I think Rosa Luxemburg would have agreed wholeheartedly.

Hannah Arendt believed that 'in the darkest of times' we should focus our hope on that which can 'illuminate' the times we live in. We shouldn't closely scrutinize only the present but 'delve into the depths of the past,' not from a nostalgic longing for the past but to better understand what is happening right now (*Men in Dark Times*, p. 58). We can turn to the thinkers and poets who came before us to focus our vision. Rebecca Solnit also emphasizes the need to study the past to move forward in an essay in the *Guardian* in 2016: 'Together we are very powerful, and we have a seldom-told, seldom-remembered history of victories and transformations that can give us confidence that, yes, we can change the world because we have many times before. You row forward looking back, and telling this history is part of helping people navigate toward the future.' Hope also means being well prepared for what hasn't yet been born and not despairing if this moment takes a little longer.

Hannah Arendt's concept of hope is connected to both the exploration of the past, which contains unfulfilled possibilities, and the 'unexpected new' yet to be born. Her concept of natality, which goes to the core of her thinking, continually gives fresh impetus to this hope. Thanks to our linguistic and creative abilities, we human beings aren't merely mortal beings but 'natal' beings, able to make a new start, or as Arendt writes in *The Human Condition*, with 'the capacity of beginning something anew.' Her concept of natality refers to a new beginning in the broadest sense of the word, whether the start of a new insight, action, initiative, or vision. She contrasted this with the concept mortality, which in her opinion pervades Western philosophy from Plato to Heidegger. Arendt preferred calling people 'natal' because this ability to begin anew profoundly distinguishes human beings from other mortal beings. She counters Heidegger's *Sein zum Tode* (being-toward-death) with *Sein zum Anfang* (being-toward-beginning), from always enduring to the possibility of starting anew. 'Men, though they must die, are not born in order to die but in order to begin,' she writes. You couldn't express things more hopefully.

'What may I hope?' is also one of Immanuel Kant's (1724–1804) core philosophical questions. In his work *Critique of Judgement* (1790) he writes: 'Voltaire said that heaven has given us two things to compensate us for the many miseries of life, hope and sleep. He might have added laughter to the list.' Hannah Arendt would certainly have concurred, but she would also have included the beauty of art, the connectedness of friendship, holding a communal conversation about the world, and the ability to start anew. For Arendt, taking a new initiative or putting a new insight into words means that people have the ability to intervene in the existing order. This implies it isn't permanently fixed or can't be completely determined and always has a certain amount of openness or space for interpretation, which is the seedbed, so to speak, of hope. Once we begin something anew in the world or tell our story afresh, thus taking into account the principle of natality, we also reveal *who* we are as unique people at that specific moment, and we develop the second core concept in Arendt's work: plurality. There is a wealth of different people in the world, with unique life stories which they can relate thanks to language, thinking and imagination.

Our first, physical birth conceals where we come from and what we are: cold facts of, for example, our sex and ethnicity. But Arendt thinks that people are always more than a sum of these facts. During our lives we also reveal to others who we are as unique people because we interpret the facts of our first birth in a specific way and testify to this in our political and cultural world. Every time we say or start something in the world, we conceal from others, as it were, what this interpretation looks like at this moment. This interpretation changes continually as it is subject to all the miniscule differences that arise in our lives and the world—in short, it depends on our personal experiences and is embedded in a specific social and cultural context. We can therefore never give a consistent and definitive answer to the question of who we are. Human beings are never finished or complete but a process of becoming, developing until their last breath.

I have always found this a liberating thought or, rather, one that creates freedom because it means I can't be reduced to the facts of, say, my sex—and then disqualified. We are dialogical beings, 'two-in-one,' as Arendt wrote in *The Life of the Mind*, who ideally can and are entitled to interpret the specificities of our first birth. That is why no representative of whichever quiddity is ever another at the same time, as the essentialist tradition in biology wanted to have us believe. A rose is a rose is a rose, as in Gertrude Stein's poem, but people are never any other at the same time because they use their thinking and imagination, as well as their personal experiences and history, to continually reinterpret the cold facts of their first birth and show themselves as 'who' to others. At least, if they are allowed to do so by society (and culture and tradition). This is where the struggle for freedom always started for Arendt: someone is free when they are empowered in a political and cultural respect to tell their story.

This conception of freedom was certainly shared by Rosa Luxemburg. Her political struggle aimed to empower the people and stimulate them to put forward their thoughts, opinions, and stories. In Arendt's essay on Isak Dinesen, in *Men in Dark Times*, she paraphrases Dinesen: 'Who are you? will be the Cardinal's answer, "Allow me . . . to answer you in the classic manner, and to tell you a story," is the only aspiration worthy of the fact that life has been given us.' In her many hundreds of letters Rosa Luxemburg repeatedly tells who she was, and she was more than happy to enlist the support of poets and writers, like her beloved Goethe. Her letters are so candid and frank that they show much more clearly who she, Rosa Luxemburg, was than her political pamphlets, which gives her letters great eloquence.

The stories we tell are rarely predictable or of a similar nature, Arendt held, not only because we all have different biographies but also because we all have the ability to start anew. She expands on this in *The Human Condition*:

> The new always happens against the overwhelming odds
> of statistical laws and their probability, which for all
> practical, everyday purposes amounts to certainty; the new

therefore always appears in the guise of a miracle. The fact that man is capable of action means that the unexpected can be expected from him, that he is able to perform what is infinitely improbable. And this again is possible only because each man is unique, so that with each birth fomenting uniquely new comes into the world. . . . The miracle that saves the world, the realm of human affairs, from its normal, 'natural' ruin is ultimately the fact of natality, in which the faculty of action is ontologically rooted. Only the full experience of this capacity can bestow upon human affairs faith and hope.

That summer in Burgundy in 2018, I started looking for philosophical concepts that could deepen my understanding of hope. It was supposed to be the sequel to *Melancholy in Times of Turmoil*. In this essay I explain how melancholy needs hope and inspiration to prevent a lapse into pure despair. But as well as discovering new ways of thinking about hope in Hannah Arendt's work, I discovered a new thinker and *mensch*: Rosa Luxemburg, who was guided by hope for an 'unexpected' better world in both her thinking and action. I grew more and more interested in this remarkable woman, who was murdered just over a century ago, during the Spartacist uprising in Berlin. Who was this originally Polish-Jewish female political thinker? And why is there such renewed interest in her work at this moment in history?

3

'The most revolutionary thing one can do always is to proclaim loudly what is happening,' Rosa Luxemburg often said, and that's exactly what she did from early childhood onward. Born on March 5, 1871, in Zamość in Russian Poland, she moved with her family to Warsaw when she was only two. She was the youngest daughter of a middle-class Jewish-Polish family committed to the values of the enlightened late eighteenth-century Haskalah movement; the Luxemburg household was filled with music, poetry, and philosophical discussions. Her early childhood was happy, but the misdiagnosis of a hip problem when she was five led to her being bedbound for a whole year, leaving her with a permanent limp.

Her biographers, from J. P. Nettl in 1966 to Dana Mills in 2020, agree that she was a brilliant pupil, exceptionally admitted as the only Jewish girl to a grammar school. She also wrote and translated poetry from a very young age, having her first literary attempts successfully published by magazines in Warsaw. At thirteen she even wrote a satirical poem about the visit of Kaiser Wilhelm I to Warsaw.

As a child, she experienced the tsarist regime's hard-handed methods; speaking Polish was forbidden at school, and all resistance was severely punished. As a Jewish Pole, she was also treated as a second-class pupil. Despite graduating with the highest grades, she wasn't awarded the gold medal 'on account of an antagonistic attitude toward the authorities,' but really because of her independent mind, sharp tongue, and Jewish background; this awoke her critical and political consciousness early on. She refused to bow to any authority that considered itself above criticism, and she was determined to make up her own mind on social and political matters.

Witnessing the poverty and wretched living conditions endured by the vast majority of people in Warsaw, she joined the Polish Proletariat Party as a fifteen-year-old and began reading Karl Marx's writings. The execution of four members of the revolutionary party made her an even more avid member of this political group. Rosa Luxemburg grew convinced that the 'class struggle' capitalism engendered between a wealthy and privileged minority and the bulk of very poor workers, soldiers, craftsmen, and civil servants would only be overcome by replacing capitalism with democratic socialism. She was never shy of voicing her opinion, and after helping to organize a general strike, she was forced to flee the country when barely eighteen, hidden under a cartload of straw. With false papers, she traveled to Zurich, a haven for Russian, Polish, and German socialists. It was also the only European city where female students were admitted to university. Toward the end of 1889, she had rooms overlooking Lake Zurich, where she loved taking afternoon strolls; she was a lifelong stroller and nature lover.

In Zurich, she graduated in philosophy, economics, and law with a dissertation on 'The Industrial Development of Poland.' Her professor had awarded her thesis the highest honors, but the university board decided this was too lofty for a woman and reduced the grade, as her friend Mathilde Jacob related in *Rosa Luxemburg: An Intimate Portrait*. It was also in Zurich where she met Leo Jogiches, a Jewish Marxist intellectual from Lithuania. They were lovers for quite some time, and perhaps Rosa had hoped for more. Jogiches was already married to the political cause, but they collaborated on political matters until Luxemburg's death. For several years, they were the core of the Socjaldemokracja Królestwa Polskiego (SDKPiL), the Social Democratic Party of Poland and Lithuania.

'Rosa's letters to Leo show the depth of her self-awareness in a relationship that knew dramatic ups and downs, but was fueled by erotic passion and intellectual fire,' as Dana Mills writes in her biography of Luxemburg. Time and again she proclaimed her love to Jogiches, but politics always eclipsed romantic love for him. She writes: 'My entire soul is filled with you, and it embraces you. . . . I want to love you. I want the same gentle, trusting, ideal atmosphere to exist between us as existed back then.' In the letters to her lover, translated by Elzbieta Ettinger in *Comrade and Lover: Letters to Leo Jogiches*, Rosa Luxemburg often reveals her most vulnerable and dependent side: 'Without meaning to, I observe everything with your eyes and take pains with every little thing and arrange it as you would, the way that would please you. When will you finally see it?' She would have loved to live with him and start a family—'Of course, I'd be happy to have you in *my home* instead of being your guest'—but the political struggle comes between them. 'The tension between her passion for Leo,' writes Dana Mills, 'her dreaming of a settled, bourgeois life, and the spark of revolution marching her onwards seems to be not easily reconciled.' Mills notes that this struggle would 'haunt women activists long after

Rosa, and yet her articulation of this contradiction is striking.' This is reflected in her letter to him in July 1897: 'You,
my dear, often understand me too superficially. You think
I'm always "sulking" because you're going away or something like that. And you can't imagine that it hurts me deeply
that for you our relationship is something totally external.'

In 1893 Luxemburg was part of the SDKPiL's delegation
at the Third Congress of the Second International in Zurich,
where she was the only female delegate. Hundreds of European socialists attended the congress, including Friedrich
Engels, French politician Jean Jaurès, German politician August Bebel, Dutch socialists Domela Nieuwenhuis and Pieter
Jelles Troelstra, as well as several representatives of social
democratic parties from around the world. Eyewitnesses
spoke of the huge impression this woman of barely twenty-
two made at the conference. She delivered an impassioned
speech on the growth of the Polish Social Democratic Party,
participating in the congress for the first time, despite its
fierce daily struggle with Russian tsarism. She emphasized
the great difference between the political struggles in various countries, contrasting how Social Democrats in the West
were freely able to achieve victory after victory, while 'we in
the East must risk our freedom and our lives for it every day.'

Belgian socialist leader Emile Vandervelde was also present at the congress and Mills quotes his recollection of her:
'I can see her now; how she sprang from among delegates
and jumped into a chair to make herself better heard. Small,
delicate and dainty in a summer dress, she advocated her
cause with such magnetism in her eyes and with such fiery
words that she enthralled and won over the great majority of
the congress, who raised their hands in favor of the accep-
tance of her mandate.' Although as a young Polish woman
she was an 'eternal outsider,' as Mills writes, 'always on un-

equal standing with others and yet demanding her voice to be heard,' she managed to convince a majority of the delegates with her sharp intelligence, her enthusiasm, and the passion and liveliness of her thoughts. 'I want to affect people like a clap of thunder,' she once wrote to Leo Jogiches, 'to inflame their minds not by speechifying but with the breadth of my vision, the strength of my conviction and the power of expression.'

This same passion and liveliness also characterizes her many letters. They are so powerfully expressed that they could have been written a few weeks rather than more than a century ago, transcending the boundaries of time. Rosa Luxemburg's letters show what Hannah Arendt called the 'track of non-time' in *The Life of the Mind*. When we think, Arendt argues, we aren't conscious of the classical Kantian conceptualization of time and space because we are in 'the in-between' where 'reality and existence, which we can only conceive in terms of time and space, can be temporarily suspended,' interrupting chronological time, which counts hours and orders events sequentially. In the 'gap between past and future we find our place in time when we think,' called the *nunc stans*, the 'standing now,' in medieval philosophy. It can be understood as the confluence of two opposing time axes in an eternal *Augenblick* (moment), which Arendt calls 'the small inconspicuous track of non-time.' 'Following that course,' Arendt writes, 'the thought-trains, remembrance and anticipation, save whatever they touch from the ruin of historical and biographical time.' This is a fascinating idea, Arendt continues, for it is quite possible that 'the strange survival of great works' is because they are conceived in the 'track of non-time' and can thus withstand the ravages of time.

Not only Rosa Luxemburg's letters but also her ideas and

thoughts have proved to be timeless after more than a century, as Jane Gordon argued at the online book launch of *Creolizing Rosa Luxemburg* on March 5, 2021, commemorating
Luxemburg's 150th birthday. In this collection of essays, a
group of renowned authors charts the many pressing political issues of her and our time, including her analysis of primitive accumulation of capital, which will be dealt with later
in this book, and her contention that capitalism, colonialism, and sexism are interrelated and as such should be tack-
led together. Several of Luxemburg's letters, handwritten
manuscripts, and postcards—as well as drawings and leaves
in her herbariums—are kept in the International Institute of
Social History archives in Amsterdam, including letters to
Luise and Karl Kautsky and to Dutch writer, poet, and socialist Henriette Roland Holst, who described her in one of the
first Luxemburg biographies, published in 1935: 'Her low,
sonorous voice, her excellent diction, her great self-control,
and the calm confidence of her conduct at a congress where
political passions repeatedly boiled over—it all made a deep
impression on me.' She also mentioned Luxemburg's 'passionate temperament,' which regularly caused clashes with
other party members, and noted her 'caustic irony and mer-
ciless mockery' but concluded that she was 'the most brilliant and bold representative of romantic socialist radical-
ism.' Luxemburg would probably have raised an eyebrow
at being called 'romantic' but would undoubtedly have ap-
preciated Roland Holst's remark that 'her innermost being
was warm humanity' and that she was 'never cruel or course
in her criticism of others, as they were to her.' Throughout
her life, Luxemburg endured immense criticism, usually of
a downright anti-Semitic or misogynist kind. But she managed to hold her own as a Jewish, Polish, and female politi-

cian in the male-dominated world of the International, relying on her knowledge, zest for life, and rhetorical skills.

After her studies, which also took her to Paris, Rosa Luxemburg married a friend, Gustav Lubeck, to gain German citizenship and move to Berlin. She settled in the German capital in 1898 and started playing a prominent role in the Social Democratic Party of Germany (SPD). She befriended German politicians like Karl Kautsky, Clara Zetkin, and Karl Liebknecht, who—like her—were on the party's left wing. She engaged in polemics with more moderate party members like Eduard Bernstein, who believed that gradual reform of capitalism could also improve workers' lot. Luxemburg didn't believe this was the solution to their immense poverty and misery because it wouldn't fundamentally alter the conventional power and production relations in the imperial and militarist German state. A series of her critical articles were published in 1899 as *Social Reform or Revolution?* While welcoming reforms, she argued they wouldn't undo the German empire's pact with capitalism.

Luxemburg asserted that giving the economy cooperative underpinnings, along with socialist 'council democracy,' with the people actually having a say and gaining political decision-making power through 'popular councils,' was the only way of thwarting capitalism's global dominance. Basing her arguments on Marx's analysis of the Paris Commune (1871), Luxemburg held that popular councils should be incorporated into parliamentary democracy. This would give people a structural means of thinking and deciding on important political policy matters. In her book *On Revolution* (1966), Hannah Arendt revived Luxemburg's proposal for citizen or popular councils, characterizing them as 'oases in a desert'; this form of direct democracy could potentially not only promote community spirit and popular political involvement but also take the wind out of extremist leaders' sails. Both Luxemburg and Arendt believed that political issues were far too important to be left solely to politicians.

These 'popular councils' would result in improved living and working conditions and an economy focused on meeting everyone's needs equitably. Capitalist production methods would be replaced by cooperative ones, with workers taking control of the production process and becoming co-owners. A model based on profit for the few would be replaced by an economy founded on shared and prudent utilization of the proceeds of goods, farmland, and labor. Production would no longer be directed toward 'the enrichment of one individual,' Luxemburg wrote in *The Socialization of Society* in 1918, but toward 'delivering to the public at large the means of satisfying all its needs.' The economy should 'have the aim of securing for everyone a dignified life, plentiful food and providing other cultural means of existence.' This would require the 'socialization' of large companies and industries, a euphemism for 'expropriation,' meaning rescinding management and shareholders' private ownership and returning it to the 'cooperative' company's workers and the larger community.

Proposals like this are unsettling to a twenty-first-century reader, with the legacy of the Soviet Union still a recent memory. At least, they are to me—but Luxemburg wrote this text long before socialism had degenerated into totalitarianism; she was in fact one of the first critics to warn of this danger. I was somewhat reassured by her qualification that 'we do not need and do not want to dispossess the small farmer and craftsman eking out a living with a small plot of land or workshop,' and 'socialization will above all extend to the large enterprises,' where the relationship between profits and workers' wages had been completely distorted. 'Only somebody who performs some useful work for the public at large, whether by hand or brain, can be entitled to receive from society the means for satisfying his needs. A life of leisure like most of the rich exploiters currently lead will come to an end. A general requirement to work for all who can do so, from which small children, the aged and sick are exempted, is a matter of course in a socialist economy. The public at large must provide forthwith for those unable to work—not like now with paltry alms but with generous provision, socialized child-raising, enjoyable care for the elderly, public health care for the sick, etc.'

Rosa Luxemburg aimed to restore people's dignity by taking them out of a sphere of inequality and poverty, as well as by restoring their autonomy over their lives and work, instead of being forced to follow management directives. 'Our dignity as working people—*notre dignité humaine*—has been taken away from us,' I heard someone say on French radio that summer in 2018. This sentiment was regularly repeated in the ensuing months. Rosa Luxemburg wrote that 'nowadays work in industry, in agriculture and in the office is mostly a torment and a burden' for workers. She reasoned that much more attention must be paid to 'the health of the workforce and its enthusiasm for work must be given the greatest consideration at work. Short working hours that do not exceed the normal capability, healthy workrooms, all methods of recuperation and a variety of work must be introduced in order that everyone enjoys doing their part.'

Luxemburg's concern for working conditions was quite

unusual at the time. She also repeatedly underlined the need for adequate rest, education, and continued self-development. At the time, rest was mostly seen as 'the devil's playground,' but Luxemburg insisted that it was a precondition of self-development. For her, being human was never a completed fact or process, in the way a product can be 'finished' or 'ready,' but rather a state of constantly becoming and developing. In other words, only through a lifelong process of learning and developing could one truly be a human being, and this required rest and sufficient time. Luxemburg always strove for the emancipation and education of all people, including the lower classes, who were increasingly alienated from themselves and their talents and abilities by the pressure of long and hard work days. Marx coined the term 'alienation' in his Paris Manuscripts in 1844, and it was taken up by Luxemburg. When humans are constantly reduced to mere cogs in an immense production process, they aren't alienated only from their work but from themselves and others too. Capitalism forces a bigger and bigger workload on workers, denying them much opportunity for self-development, and it forces them to compete with each other, alienating them from their human nature, which is essentially social.

As well as transforming a capitalist model into a form of social democracy, Luxemburg argued that the arts and knowledge of nature and science were an important counterweight to this alienation. 'It is not only those who lack food who are alienated and humiliated,' she wrote, 'but also those who lack claim to the great gifts of humankind.' She firmly believed that art and poetry should no longer be a bourgeois privilege but an emotional and intellectual experience for all. Luxemburg was also convinced that literature could contribute to revolutionary change. For instance, she wrote in her review of Frans Mehring's 1917 biography of Schiller that 'the spread of Schiller's poetry across the proletarian layers of Germany has, without doubt, contributed to his intellectual and revolutionizing elevation, and has to that extent played its part in the work of the emancipation of the working class.' In her letters, she often describes the soothing and healing effect poetry and music had on her, as in this moving passage about Goethe's poetry in a letter from prison to her friend Sonja Liebknecht (1917): 'It was only the music of the words and the strange magic of the poem which lulled me into tranquility. I don't know why it is myself that a beautiful poem, especially by Goethe, so deeply affects me on every moment of strong excitement or emotion. The effect is almost physical. It's as if with parched lips I was sipping a delicious drink that cools my spirit and heals me, body and soul.'

4

While I was absorbed in Rosa Luxemburg's work in Burgundy, the popular uprising in France took on more serious proportions in early autumn. Farmers dumped bales of hay on the roads, and the odd town hall was daubed with milk or fertilizer; we're used to scenes like this in the French countryside. But within a couple of days, the roundabouts in our region, the Nièvre, were occupied by countless gilets jaunes. From one day to the next, the local population had spontaneously donned yellow vests, which the government had made compulsory in cars in France two years earlier—a measure it must have rued many times in the last few years. To be honest, we didn't really know what to make of it all. The French press initially reported that the protesters were right-wing or populist rioters, but that was soon revised, although it took some time for certain newspapers and media—local and foreign—to do so.

Without any trade union or political party leadership, barricades were erected across France, blocking access to major roads and highways. On the roundabouts, people warmed themselves companionably by fires in oil drums, doled out coffee and sandwiches, and as the resistance continued, Christmas trees were put up here and there for some cheer. 'On se retrouve enfin,' one of my neighbors sighed with a smile; torn away from their televisions and lonely cottages, people reconnected around the makeshift fires. Our first impression of the revolt in the countryside was of a convivial uprising, but things were rougher in the cities. In Paris and other big cities like Marseille, Bordeaux, and Toulouse the protest resulted in large demonstrations on many successive Saturdays, at which hundreds of *casseurs*—stone throwers—fought pitched battles with police and other French 'security services,' including the Compagnies républicaines de sécurité, the general reserve of the French National Police. Despite shops and cars being destroyed, most of the public supported the demonstrations. 'What is this violence compared to the extreme violence of social domination, of poverty?' Édouard Louis asked rhetorically in an interview with the *New Yorker* (December 15, 2018).

A few years earlier, in 2014, Louis's novel *The End of Eddy*, about growing up in Hallencourt, a small town in northern France, was published. He chronicles a world scarred by unemployment, poverty, violence, prejudice, and pain. Like many nearby villages and towns in the immense French countryside, his native region has endured the consequences of globalized capitalism, which has throttled artisanship and small-scale trade and agriculture by rendering it economically unviable. Government cutbacks have continued apace, with many public facilities and services being slashed. As on the other side of the Channel, the anger and frustration of a large share of the French population has translated into votes for the extreme right Rassemblement national. The principal character in the novel, Eddy Bellegueule (Louis's original surname, which he later changed), is homosexual and is regularly called names, beaten up, and humiliated, even by his father and family. He goes to study in Amiens, which proves his salvation.

But when the yellow jacket protests erupted, Louis championed the inhabitants of Hallencourt, who also joined demonstrations in Paris. He expressed his frustration on Twitter that the grievances of the gilets jaunes had met only with sensationalism by the press and disdain by politicians. 'Something about the extreme violence and class contempt that is being unleashed on this movement paralyzes me,' he wrote in the *New Yorker*. In an interview with Alexandra Schwartz, Louis gave a poignant description of the gilets jaunes movement and explained why he had decided to join:

> I saw very poor people, people like my mother, people like my father, exhausted people, extremely poor people. I was able to read it on their faces, because I know those people. I recognized, suddenly, a *body*, in the noblest sense of the term. A body that I'm not used to seeing in the media. And I felt that these images were crying out to me. There was the emergence of the kind of body that we never see or hear. People are saying, 'I can't manage to feed myself, or my family.' And, for me, a sentence like that is so much more political, so much more powerful, than all of this discourse about 'the Republic,' the 'people,' 'coexistence,' 'democracy.' . . . It's the body of social exclusion. It's the body of people who are living in precarity, people from the North of France, or from the South of France, who come from the kinds of families that haven't gotten an education in five generations—families like mine. I grew up in a family of seven, and we had to live on seven hundred euros a month. . . . When I was a kid, my parents, and especially

my mother, always said, 'No one is talking about us. No one cares about us.' One of the most violent feelings we had was this feeling of not existing in the public discourse, in the eyes and voices of others. . . . As soon as the gilets jaunes emerged, a huge part of the political field and the media was trying to shut them down. . . . When you suffer from poverty, from exclusion, from constant humiliation, you are just trying to find a way to say, 'I suffer.'

Not only writers like Édouard Louis and many other artists but also secondary school students, university students, and teachers—Les stylos rouges, the red pens!—had joined the spontaneous demonstrations by then. Demonstrators explicitly presented themselves as an independent protest movement, avoiding association with any specific political party. 'The yellow vest movement doesn't belong to anyone and so belongs to everyone,' was their motto. The uprising may have been sparked by yet another fuel price hike, but within weeks it developed into a *révolution des citoyens*, a citizens' revolution, which renounced faith and confidence in the French Fifth Republic's political institutions. In addition to the government's resignation, they demanded an increase in the minimum wage, tax on the polluting aviation industry, reintroduction of the wealth tax, and political participation through citizens' initiative referendums and 'citizen councils.'

In the ensuing months other protest movements joined the yellow vests, including the anti-racism movement, action groups against cuts in education and the public sector, and environmental groups. This motley assortment of protesters expressed widespread social dissatisfaction with the neoliberal policies espoused by France's ruling political elite. I watched the images on French television, listened to French radio, read commentary in French newspapers, and was amazed to see how, in a few short weeks, the uprising unfolded exactly in line with Rosa Luxemburg's revolutionary analyses. Precisely fifty years after the last large-scale uprising in France, the student revolt of May 1968, people had once more taken to the barricades across the country. As the demonstrations proliferated and television debates grew more heated—'What's happening to us?' writer Christine Angot exclaimed in despair—I read more of Luxemburg's writings, looking for an answer to that very question.

In her text *The Mass Strike,* published in 1906, Rosa Luxemburg emphasized that 'the masses' seldom mobilize because of appeals by leaders of political parties or organizations, acting 'spontaneously' only when their sense of justice has been violated for too long, and resistance is sparked off spontaneously and usually unexpectedly. Demonstrations, strikes, and other political gatherings must arise from popular will and initiative, she believed, as this is the sole condition in which they give expression to political freedom and have any chance of succeeding. Only during uprisings do people learn to organize themselves in 'popular councils' or other communal groups, and then they can join preexisting trade unions or parties on their own terms.

'It was exactly the opposite of what the trade union leaders had always argued,' Dutch politician Jacques de Kadt wrote in the introduction to the first Dutch edition of Rosa Luxemburg's letters in 1976. 'The size of the union was not decisive for the action, rather the action was decisive for the growth of the trade union movement.' A lesson that trade unions nowadays, with their drastically reduced membership, should take to heart, as should contemporary activists, who lack sufficient trade union support. 'The task of trade unions and politicians is not to control and direct the start of an uprising, but its end' is one of Luxemburg's famous assertions in her famous work *The Mass Strike*. The success of current protest movements, like climate activists or Black Lives Matter, will largely depend on their capacity to self-organize and the support they then obtain from more mainstream political institutions.

In the revolutionary autumn of 2018—and succeeding months—one of the most important questions was whether the popular uprising in France was capable of this kind of self-organization. It became clear more than a year later that this was regrettably not yet the case, but the struggle for socioeconomic justice and greater civic participation isn't over in France or any other European country; social discontent is too great and widespread for that—for which there are many reasons, I wholeheartedly concede.

Almost a quarter of the European population, about 100 million people, lives on or below the poverty line, according to research by the European Commission, Oxfam, Index Mundi, and others—with extremes in Greece, Italy, and Bulgaria. Social geographer Emmanuel Todd has calculated that about half of the French population lives on a minimum income or social security. If we also include the 'precariat'— the term coined by British economist Guy Standing for the growing ranks of the self-employed and workers with temporary contracts with almost no labor rights or social security entitlements—the potential number of Europeans living in poverty and insecurity is even larger. Dutch economist Mirjam de Rijk pointed out at the end of 2018 that 'the wages of ordinary workers have hardly risen in recent years, unlike companies and financial institutions' profits.' The 'neoliberal course' that has been pursued for decades in Europe and other parts of the world has seriously undermined the position of workers and strengthened the hand of employers and capital owners.

One of the most striking conclusions from these studies is that the financial crisis of 2008–2009 hardly dented corporate profits, while workers' incomes declined sharply in most countries. In other words, the cost of bailing out the banks was passed on to the public and the public sector, resulting in cutbacks in education, health care, infrastructure, and social security. 'We are back in the nineteenth century,' Dutch economic historian Bas van Bavel argues, 'because the price of capital and labor has been left entirely to the market.' Scaling up to eradicate competition, monopolist companies, wage moderation, and eroding labor rights with flexible contracts—all are common practice.

5

The increasing concentration of power and wealth were also the subject of Rosa Luxemburg's opus magnum *The Accumulation of Capital*, written a century earlier, in 1913. It took her only four months to write this impressive and rigorous analysis of socioeconomic inequality, violence, and oppression in capitalist society. Her analysis received great praise, establishing her name in many political and economic circles. One of its conclusions is that capitalism won't necessarily be overcome through a dialectical struggle with the proletariat, as Marx had theorized. Instead, it will continue its geographical expansion indefinitely, Luxemburg thought, because it is based on an economic model of growth and expansion. Capitalist growth, she argued, requires continual extension into noncapitalist spheres: 'Accumulation is more than an internal relationship between the branches of capitalist economy; it is primarily a relationship between capital and a noncapitalist environment.' Capitalism will lead to protracted trade wars over territories, raw materials, and cheap labor, Luxemburg argued, until the entire world is exploited for capitalist purposes, with terrible consequences for humans and the environment. This analysis proved to be a prophetic warning. 'Capitalism, as a result of its own inner contradictions, [is moving] toward a point when it will be unbalanced,' she wrote, and from a geographical perspective, 'it will simply become impossible.'

Marx theorized that all labor would eventually become wage labor measured by clock time, producing one of the forms of capitalist surplus value. Profit was earned, among other things, from the difference between the average time labor takes and the minimum time required, forcing workers to do more and more work in fewer and fewer hours. Clock time became, so to speak, one of the driving forces behind capitalist society, as I have discussed at length in my other books, for example, *Stil de tijd* (Time on Our Side) and *Kairos*. Despite all the time-saving devices we have developed in the last century, I argue that we are always in a hurry, feel stressed, and experience a structural lack of time because of these capitalist dynamics.

Until the adoption of the international time standard in Greenwich in 1884, local time, usually based on astronomical observations, determined the patterns of our daily lives. This was a time based on both the habits of a community and the change of the seasons with its corresponding cycles of sowing and harvesting. The new, international clock time was, as you might say, superimposed on these local times to become the world's overarching structuring principle. You might even say that the introduction of Greenwich Mean Time marked the start of globalization and humankind's alienation from its local and natural rhythm. The industrialization of society and the ensuing introduction of factory whistles and time clocks reinforced this trend. Instead of living in some degree of harmony with time, human life came to be ruled by the clock as I explain in my previous essays on time. Over the course of the twentieth century, humankind became locked in a struggle with time, brilliantly portrayed by Charlie Chaplin in the film *Modern Times* in 1936. In this film, the man with the bowler hat is in danger of being literally devoured by the accelerating machines, while his humanity seems to be crushed by the ruthless regime of the clock that keeps increasing the pace of production. In the end he almost turns into a machine himself. *Modern Times* was Chaplin's answer to the futurist manifesto of Filippo Marinetti, who extolled speed and embraced the acceleration of time—'a racing car is more beautiful than the Nike of Samothrace'—and acclaimed the achievements of the industrial era. Chaplin wanted his film to show that if time is seen as merely working time, as a production quota to be met, humankind becomes alienated from itself.

Over the course of the twentieth century working hours became juxtaposed with hard-won 'leisure time.' Strangely enough, this nonwork time is now also increasingly spent on activities: foreign travel, survival trips, and other 'active holidays' are immensely popular. The keenness with which travel is being taken up again in the West in 2021, with terms like 'revenge travel,' suggest that even a global pandemic will do little to deter this development in the long term. Even in our leisure time, it seems, time mustn't be empty and should be 'filled' to bursting. At the slightest hint of boredom, we immediately switch to our next moment of excitement, as though rest and unoccupied time have become so alien to us that they fill us with dread. We have also come to experience time as something increasingly scarce. Despite all our new time-saving devices, we are left with less and less time for rest and relaxation. The faster we can travel, the less time we have to stay anywhere. The more accessible we are by mobile phone, email, or internet, the less time we have for one another. Whereas a letter used to take a day or two to reach us, nowadays we are supposed to reply to an email within an hour. All of this has reinforced the perception of time as being in short supply.

Who owns time? Is our time still our own? There is little to suggest it is. Time has long since ceased to be a private matter. In contemporary society, time is mostly regulated from outside, externally imposed economic time is the rule. Besides, capitalist ideology continually seduces us into accelerating our consumption. Dutch sociologist Anton Zijderveld dubs this 'staccato culture.' Constantly motivated by capitalist impulses, we want more, we want the latest, and we want it now. It is no exaggeration to say capitalism governs time and therefore also our private lives and inner experience of time.

Anyone who consults the many future scenarios commissioned by Western governments and corporations around the turn of the millennium will come away with a less-than-rosy picture of what the next fifty years will bring us. Social divisions are expected to widen, the threat of terror is forecast to increase, and the effects of climate change will become ever more extreme. Historic city centers and pleasant suburbs will be home to more affluent, highly educated citizens, who, when not floored by stress or burnout, will work flat out and protect their properties with fences and CCTV cameras. Impoverished urban peripheries and rural areas will be inhabited by large groups of unemployed people and illegal immigrants, unable to find jobs in the knowledge economy. The entire population will be in the grip of growing unrest and insecurity caused by increasing societal complexity and accelerating technological change. In short, the experience awaiting us—and which is already gathering momentum—is a sense of time running out. On the one hand, we must act swiftly if we want to limit the effects of climate change. On the other, there is increasing pressure to step up production and innovation to keep the economy on track. We appear to have reached an impasse at the start of the twenty-first century: the climate demands less, the economy more; humankind wants to slow down, society to speed up.

That time is first and foremost a political and economic construct serving neoliberal or capitalist ideas is an opinion shared by Alain Badiou. In his 2004 book *The Century*, the French philosopher argues that this ideology has led to an extreme form of individualism, which has adopted 'the unrestrained pursuit of self-interest' as its motto. For all the per capita growth of the Western economy over the past century, we are all familiar with the other side of the coin: unequal distribution of wealth, depletion of natural resources, and sharply increasing waves of economic and climate refugees. On a more existential level, Badiou believes that this individualism has led to the steady decline in public spiritedness and solidarity, as well as to an increase in fundamental loneliness

Time is one of the pillars of our existence. We shouldn't forget that how we think about time is indicative of how we think about ourselves and the world. The global economic downturn, the pandemic, and the impending climate crisis may actually give us the opportunity to liberate time from the capitalist straightjacket we have forced it into. In short, it is time to put rest and contemplation, alongside with solidarity and public spiritedness, back on the political agenda. Without these prerequisites for reflection, loneliness won't become just a new Western pandemic, it will also threaten Western democracy itself.

In *The Accumulation of Capital*, Rosa Luxemburg described

how nonwage labor or underpaid labor could also contribute to capitalist profit, referring to the unpaid labor of slaves and colonized peoples in her time, which we now call offshoring: outsourcing labor to 'low-wage countries.' In other words, Luxemburg added a 'spatial' and geographical argument to the Marxist analysis of wage labor, primitive accumulation, and the 'time is money' principle. She even viewed the necessity of continuous geographic expansion of capitalist areas for cheap production, labor, and markets as the core of this dynamic: imperialism isn't a free choice but a capitalist law. Luxemburg gives many examples of capitalist countries exploiting labor from noncapitalist societies: 'For the first genuinely capitalist branch of production, the English cotton industry, not only the cotton of the Southern states of the American Union was essential, but also the millions of African Negroes who were shipped to America to provide the labor power for the plantations.'

Her meticulous study of the capitalist cycle of production, market, and growth made Luxemburg one of the first people to recognize that this economic system relied on the colonization of 'noncapitalist countries' to sustain itself. She remarked as early as 1913 that imperialism and colonialism don't take place on the theoretical periphery, as Marx suggested, but at the center: 'Imperialism is the political expression of capital accumulation.' It also explains her book's original subtitle, omitted in some translations: *A Contribution to the Explanation of Imperialism*. Luxemburg explicitly compares the expropriation of medieval European peasants and the destructive power of 'modern colonial politics.' *The Rosa Luxemburg Reader* (2004) contains several other texts on slavery, including a newspaper article about a volcanic eruption on the French island colony Martinique. She exposes the hypocrisy of European countries' desire to help victims of natural disasters while failing to recognize how for centuries they have oppressed and expropriated these same people with colonial violence. Her historical analysis of capitalism fully considered slavery, colonial exploitation, and the destruction of social communities and original economies. In her view, they were indispensable complements to western capitalism.

In an early text, *Introduction to Political Economy*, her unfinished book begun in 1908, Rosa Luxemburg pointed out that socialism could never be confined to only a single country since no political economy can exist in isolation; 'How are we to draw borders between the economy of one nation and that of another?' She showed instead the interdependence between world economies in commodities, labor, and production: 'Within each industrial country, capitalist production ceaselessly drives out pretty trade, handcraft and small peasant production. At the same time it draws all backward European countries, and the lands of America, Asia, Africa and Australia, into the world economy. This happens in two ways: by world trade and by colonial conquests.' Rosa Luxemburg was therefore 'one of the first Marxists who developed a truly global concept of solidarity,' as Dutch historian Marcel van der Linden argues in his essay 'Rosa Luxemburg's Global Class Analysis' in *Historical Materialism* (2016).

The insight that capitalism always needs something outside itself for its growth and hence continued existence was described by Hannah Arendt in her essay on Luxemburg as 'genius.' It shed new light on colonialist regimes and was adopted by Arendt in her famous analysis in *The Origins of Totalitarianism* (1951). Rosa Luxemburg considered the necessity of growth and expansive compulsion inherent to capitalism—resulting in negligent management of energy resources, destruction of the natural environment, and serious environmental pollution. That capitalism would also manage to find a vast range of new noncapitalist spheres to exploit in the private domain, for example, thanks to the commercialization of care and education and the large-scale sale of internet and privacy data, is something neither Luxemburg nor Arendt could have foreseen. But Luxemburg did recognize as early as 1913 that 'capitalism is the first mode of economy with the weapon of propaganda, a mode which tends to engulf the entire globe and to stamp out all other economies, tolerating no rival at its side.'

Internet companies like Google and Facebook have penetrated our private domains with a new form of capitalism, writes Harvard economist Shoshana Zuboff in her book *The Age of Surveillance Capitalism* (2019). They offer free internet services but methodically monitor our behavior, selling this data without our permission to advertisers and other enterprises. These companies not only violate our privacy and other rights, like copyright and intellectual property, but also acquire power over and knowledge about us without any democratic control, which is used to increase their profits—and those of the political and commercial buyers of this data. In Zuboff's opinion, 'surveillance capitalism' undermines the rule of law and democracy. Every aspect of our lives, including our medical files and résumés, has fallen into their clutches thanks to the complete digitization of personal information. 'We once searched Google,' Zuboff remarked in an interview with the *Guardian* on January 20, 2019, 'but now Google searches us.'

As capitalism can hardly grow geographically, the necessary expansion has shifted to our private lives, as well as to public-sector health care and education. In the 1980s, several

German researchers from the Bielefeld School connected this to market encroachment of the private sphere through the commercialization of women's bodies: the 'birth market' related to procreation—including surrogacy and adoption, which economically vulnerable women are forced into—and other medical practices. This also includes the pharmaceutical industry's power and the marketization of health care; they are all 'noncapitalist areas' that have been subjugated to free-market thinking, with all its consequences. This capitalist expansion, aimed purely at short-term profit and economic returns, is at odds with citizens' interests.

'Currently all wealth . . . belongs to a few Junkers [landowners] and private capitalists,' Luxemburg wrote in *The Socialization of Society* in 1918. A century later, and not much has changed. 'The great mass of the workers only get a meagre wage to live on for hard work.' The whole production process 'is conducted by individual capitalists on their own initiative,' Luxemburg continues. 'What—and in which way—is to be produced, where, when and how the produced goods are to be sold is determined by the industrialist. The workers do not see to all this, they are just living machines who have to carry out their work.' She concludes that 'the enrichment of a small number of idlers is the aim of today's economy.' Accumulation of capital by the few, 'accumulation of dispossession' for many others, as British economic geographer and City University of New York professor David Harvey, a great admirer of Luxemburg's work, describes it. 'Dividends rise and the working class falls' as Luxemburg bluntly put it.

While Luxemburg's language may sometimes sound a little dated, her analysis is, again, germane: 'The super-rich lose billions on falling stock markets,' newspaper head-lines screamed in December 2018. Stock markets around the world had fallen about 10 percent by the end of the year, and newspapers calculated that 'the planet's 500 richest people [had] lost a total of about 451 billion dollars.' The sums are so absurdly astronomical that even Rosa Luxemburg proba-bly couldn't have imagined them. The World Economic Fo-rum in Davos reported in 2019 that economic inequality was increasing across the globe. One of the assembled multi-billionaires, American Ray Dalio, who owns Bridgewater Associates hedge fund, announced to the assembled media that 'capitalism,' to which he owed his eye-watering fortune of 18 billion dollars, 'basically is not working for the major-ity of people' and that inequality was only going to increase in the coming years.

And so 'the tide of hypercapitalism has to be turned!' French economist Thomas Piketty exclaimed in a debate on French television. Piketty shot to international fame with his book *Capital in the Twenty-First Century*, in which he fol-lows in Rosa Luxemburg's footsteps by expounding the un-equal accumulation of capital as one of the biggest problems facing society, regrettably without a single reference to her magnum opus. Strangely enough, he has also stated in inter-views, perhaps for strategic reasons, that he has never been able to read Marx. Piketty argues that if capitalism isn't re-strained, once again echoing Luxemburg, it won't lead just to an ever-increasing concentration of wealth but also to po-litical unrest, large-scale migration, and trade wars, such as the one the United States and China are currently mired in. Stewardship of the climate and the environment is also se-riously threatened as industry—focused on growth—is loath to take responsibility.

Both Luxemburg and Piketty proposed new systems of wealth taxes and redistribution of capital and means of production, to which I will return, while Macron's government did the exact opposite in the summer of 2018 by abolishing the French wealth tax. Piketty expressed his outrage about this on French television with the yellow vests, who had been chanting for weeks on roundabouts 'Fin du mois, fin du monde.' The fight against the economic injustice of people lacking the money to make 'the end of the month' goes together with the fight against global warming or 'the end of the world.' Yet, capital taxes are no panacea. We will also have to think about a more fundamental renewal of the economic system and discuss the possibilities of collective political action. Although the French gilets jaunes revolt foundered after protesting for seventy Saturdays in a row, it cannot be denied that, at the very least, it attempted to do just that.

It is only recently that Luxemburg's most important work, *The Accumulation of Capital,* has received the interest it deserves as an economic, political, and philosophical work. It was denounced by the Left and the Right, either for not obediently following Marxist doctrine or for being interested in Marxism at all. Researchers around the world are now recognizing this work as one of the most important political and economic analyses of the twentieth century. Luxemburg greatly enjoyed writing the book, as her biographer Paul Frohlich noted, and she delighted in understanding what was going on:

> The time when I was writing the [first] *Accumulation of Capital* belongs to the happiest of my life. Really I was living as though in euphoria, 'on a high,' saw and heard

nothing else, day or night, but this one question, which unfolded before me so beautifully, and I don't know what to say about which gave me the greater pleasure: the process of thinking, when I was turning a complicated problem over in my mind, pacing slowly back and forth through the room, under the close and attentive observation of Mimi [the cat], who lay on the red plush tablecloth with her little paws curled under her and kept turning her wise head back and forth to follow my movements; or the process of giving shape and literary form to my thoughts with pen in hand. Do you know, at that time I wrote the whole [thing] all at one go in four months' time—an unprecedented event!—and without rereading [the rough draft], not even once, I sent it off to be printed.

6

Rosa Luxemburg and Hannah Arendt were both critical, female thinkers, deeply involved in the political events of the twentieth century. They both suffered under violent political regimes and shared a lifelong sense of urgency to rethink the nature of political systems of power and alienation. Although they were temporally separated by the Second World War and the rise of totalitarianism, they both developed a concept of freedom that can be understood as an active and critical participation in public life. They also challenged the authority of male domination of politics and philosophy: Luxemburg by criticizing the ideas of Bernstein and Lenin; Arendt by commenting critically on the way her celebrated teacher and former lover, Martin Heidegger, embraced National Socialism. Although they never declared themselves feminists, they certainly acted in a feminist vein. It was also some time before the world took note of their political and philosophical genius and recognized it as such, ironically thanks to the development of feminist thought.

Hannah Arendt's writings have been discovered on a larger, international scale since the 1980s, but interest in Rosa Luxemburg's work is far more recent. For a long time she was, as Hannah Arendt correctly notes in *Men in Dark Times*, 'the most controversial and least understood figure in the German Left movement.' She continued: 'It was precisely success—success even in her own world of revolutionaries—which was withheld from Rosa Luxemburg in life, death and after death.' Rosa Luxemburg wasn't a marginal figure of the Left, but a marginalized protagonist in the history of twentieth-century political thought. Male socialist leaders were sarcastic and scathing about their female colleague both during her life and after her death. She was accused of making 'ludicrous mistakes,' as Bukharin stated in his review of *The Accumulation of Capital*; her arguments were 'a farce' and she was tangled in 'a net of contradictions.'

This is probably due to Rosa Luxemburg's 'irritating willingness to question many of the necessary truths of Marxist theory,' as Andrea Nye puts it in her book *Philosophia: The Thought of Rosa Luxemburg, Simone Weil, and Hannah Arendt*. Socialist revolution was a long process of advancement and reversal, Luxemburg argued, 'and the class struggle between proletariat and bourgeoisie was not the contradiction that would bring down capitalism all together.' Luxemburg criticized several aspects of Marxist doctrine, such that also Hannah Arendt was forced to concede 'that she was not an orthodox Marxist, so little orthodox indeed that it might be doubted that she was a Marxist at all,' an interesting view to which I will return later in this book. Yet her critical assessment of Marxist doctrine does partly explain her male colleagues' disdain.

Renewed interest in Rosa Luxemburg's work shows that contemporary readers, including Jane Gordon and Drucilla Cornell (2021), Dana Mills (2020), Jacqueline Rose (2014), and myself, firmly reject the idea that she made 'ludicrous mistakes.' She rightly predicted not only the ongoing rise in socioeconomic inequality across the world but also the in-

terconnectedness of capitalism, imperialism, and colonialism, and the threat of escalating environmental and climatic
problems. Increasing resistance to global capitalism and the
quest for meaningful political and economic alternatives
also explain the renewed interest in her work. Rosa Luxemburg believed that capitalism was a transitory phase, which
could only be transformed into a cooperative economic
model with the help of the critical consciousness of the majority of the population, instead of a handful political leaders and party members, and the political self-organization
of the people in *Volksrade,* or citizens' councils. She was a political thinker who wanted to use her studies of society, politics, and economics to both educate the people and show
them that collective resistance and civic disobedience were
possible. Her goal wasn't power for the party but everybody's
political freedom to express their views and participate in
political decisions, similar to what Hannah Arendt had in
mind when she discussed the popular councils in Paris and
Hungary in her book *On Revolution.*

Rosa Luxemburg's freedom of expression was curbed
more and more after *The Accumulation of Capital* was published in 1913, as the SPD's left wing—which also included
Karl Liebknecht and Clara Zetkin—grew increasingly es-
tranged from more moderate party members, who couldn't
bring themselves to voice approval of her book. According
to Hannah Arendt, only Franz Mehring was 'unprejudiced
enough to call it a "truly magnificent, fascinating achievement without its equal since Marx's death."' Nor did the
Social Democrats want to risk their newly acquired political power for uncertain radical political changes like a democracy based upon citizens' councils and, in Luxemburg's
words, tended instead toward conformity 'on the parquet

floor of bourgeois parliamentarism.' Their argument that gradual reform would contain capitalism in the long run was rejected by both Luxemburg and Karl Liebknecht. But the party's willingness to support the kaiser's decision to go to war was the main cause of a complete breakdown in relations.

Luxemburg and Liebknecht concluded on August 4, 1914, that the SPD hadn't just failed but had destroyed itself as a socialist party. On that fatal day, the party agreed to approve war credits for the kaiser's armies, effectively acquiescing to war on France. Biographers describe it as the darkest day in Rosa Luxemburg's life. J. P. Nettl writes that 'Luxemburg and Zetkin suffered nervous prostration, and at one moment were close to suicide.' Luxemburg couldn't possibly accept the SPD's decision because it was totally at odds with the ideal of social democratic fraternity: 'Proletarians of all countries unite in peacetime but cut each other's throats in war,' she wrote bitterly. Luxemburg predicted that the war would be an unprecedented catastrophe because developments in military technology and the scale of the conflict would decimate both the International and countless members of the working class. 'That the party [the SPD] and the International have gone kaput, thoroughly kaput, is not open to any doubt,' she wrote on November 1, 1914, to her friend Hans Diefenbach, who was killed by a grenade at the front several years later, 'but precisely the increasing dimensions of the disaster have made of it a world-historical drama.'

Her words were prophetic, I would say. In Germany alone, the war caused over eight million deaths, about 90 percent of which were from the working class. Rosa Luxemburg had tried to convince her party since the International Socialist Congress in Stuttgart in 1907 that a world war, which she regarded primarily as a capitalist war between imperialist powers, should be avoided at all costs. France, Germany, Austria-Hungary, Britain, and Russia were vying for colonized territories, raw materials, and cheap labor and expanding their economic power. In the *Junius Pamphlet* (1915) she forensically analyzed the war: 'The occurrence at Sarajevo only furnished the immediate pretext. Causes and conflicts for the war had been overripe for a long time. . . . And, indeed, not the "existence and the independent development of Germany in this war are at stake, . . . but the immediate profits of the Deutsche Bank in Asiatic Turkey and the future profits of the Mannesmann and Krupp interests in Morocco, . . . " as the *Vorwärts* wrote.' Even when the war was in full swing, she carried on calling for 'the overcoming of war and the speediest possible enforcement of peace.'

At the end of January 1917, she wrote to Luise Kautsky from prison:

> But when the whole world is out of joint, then I merely seek to understand what is going on and why, and then I have done my duty, and I am calm and in good spirits from then on. . . . This giving oneself up completely to the headaches and miseries of the day is completely incomprehensible and intolerable to me. See, for example, how Goethe stood above things with cool composure. But think what he must have gone through: the Great French Revolution, . . . an unbroken series of wars, when once again the world must have seemed like a madhouse turned loose. Yet at the same time how calmly, with such equanimity, he pursued his studies. . . . I don't ask that you be a poet like Goethe, but

everyone can adopt for themselves his outlook on life—the
universalism of interests, the inner harmony—or at least
strive toward that. . . . I embrace you, your R.

Rosa Luxemburg was finally released from prison in November 1918, a few weeks after a popular uprising had broken out in Germany. Mutinous soldiers in Kiel had refused
to take part in yet another of the kaiser's desperate offen-
sives, and their resistance had spread to other cities, where
large groups of workers had joined the strike. This led to the
toppling of the kaiser on November 9, and power was transferred to the SPD leader, Friedrich Ebert. The Luxemburg
biographies by Henriette Roland Holst (1935) and J. P. Nettl
(1966) describe the following events, which are the subject of
intense historical debate. Another SPD leader, Philip Schnei-
demann, proclaimed the German Republic from the Reichstag on November 9. Instead of being met with jubilation,
however, the confidence of protesters and activists in the
new government was at rock bottom after four years of war.
So, Karl Liebknecht proclaimed the 'Free Socialist Republic'
from the Berliner Stadtschloss palace a little later the same
day, urging the population to revolt against the new government. The revolutionary spirit spread across the starving
and war-ravaged country, as it descended into anarchy. In
Berlin and other German cities, hundreds of thousands of
people put down tools and took to the streets. They wanted
to settle accounts with the politicians who had led them into
a disastrous and protracted world war.

From the moment of her release, Rosa Luxemburg la-
bored tirelessly to steer the uprising onto the right track,
which was a Herculean task. Unlike Liebknecht and other
members of the Spartacus League—formerly the SPD's left

wing—she had serious misgivings about the timing of the revolution because she thought the chaos, problems, and war-induced poverty were too great to enlist enough popular support. Revolutionary groups were also involved in increasingly bloody skirmishes with Freikorps, counterrevolutionary paramilitary groups in the government's pay. In an effort to calm the ranks, Luxemburg wrote articles for *Die Rote Fahne* (The Red Flag newspaper) every day: 'We want the reorganization of society to take place peacefully.' Gatherings were organized on Berlin's squares, where one of the many spectators was Dutch poet Herman Gorter, who believed that 'the new spring' of international fraternity would soon take hold. He had placed all his hope in the German revolution since the pitiful failure of the Dutch revolution.

The revolutionary spirit sweeping across Europe just after the First World War even reached the Netherlands, no doubt to the surprise of many. Dutch soldiers had mutinied a few weeks earlier, and the Dutch government became increasingly afraid that the German revolution would cross the border. Its fear was justified, as the Social Democratic Workers' Party, the SDAP, called on workers to seize power on November 11. Two days later, prominent socialists Domela Nieuwenhuis and poet Henriette Roland Holst, a close friend of Rosa Luxemburg, delivered important speeches in a packed Diamond Exchange on Weesperplein Square in Amsterdam, where many thousands of people, including several hundred soldiers, had been waiting in a combative mood for two days. Convinced that the revolution had started, the throng of workers, sailors, soldiers, and other sympathizers made their way to the calvary barracks, where they called on the soldiers to join them. But military police in concealed positions began firing at the demonstrators; people were injured and killed, the crowd scattered and fled. The next day, the government sent large numbers of loyal military troops to Amsterdam, deterring demonstrators from taking to the streets, and the 'revolution' was put down in little more than twenty-four hours.

The chaos in Germany, by contrast, went on for more than two months and became such a threat to the SPD government in Berlin in the first weeks of 1919 that it decided to use propaganda and violence to crush the uprising—consisting of many of its own former supporters. 'Spartacus League commits Atrocities,' screamed the headlines in pro-government newspapers; 'Spartacus League to blame for Everything!' Yet Luxemburg and Liebknecht refused to lose hope. Instead of fleeing Berlin, 'they carried on, as bravely as ever, battling on and trying to counter the pogrom-like atmosphere at public meetings,' wrote Henriette Roland Holst, who followed the German revolution closely from the Netherlands. But she added, 'That they still thought any such thing possible proves that they had not correctly assessed the situation.' This is undoubtedly true, but we could also argue that Luxemburg had little choice. While disagreeing with the timing of the revolution, she was reluctant to abandon the people who had put their faith in her and Liebknecht.

Even though the uprising in Berlin was effectively over a few weeks later, on January 15, 1919, Rosa Luxemburg and Karl Liebknecht were taken from their beds by the protofascist Freikorps, consisting of former soldiers from the Imperial Army, who had helped the government quell the Spartacists. They were brought to Hotel Eden in Berlin. 'At the time of her arrest,' wrote Henriette Roland Holst, based on eyewitness accounts, 'we see her as Mrs. Markussohn described her. The dark rings under her eyes after all the long nights betrayed the physical tension; yet her spirit was unshaken.

She calmly packed the things she thought she would need into a small bag: some linen, toiletries, a book.' Goethe's *Faust* was the book Rosa Luxemburg took on her last journey through Berlin. 'Calmly and undaunted she took leave of her hostess and accompanied the escort to the car.' Luxemburg still thought she was only being arrested and returned to prison.

In Hotel Eden, Luxemburg and Liebknecht were interrogated under torture by the Cavalry Guards, commanded by Waldemar Pabst, before being taken away in waiting cars. 'Outside the hotel, Petty Officer Runge struck her on the back of the head with his rifle butt,' Roland Holst wrote. 'She collapsed and they lifted her into the car. During the ride she still showed signs of life now and then.' 'Don't shoot' were reputedly Rosa Luxemburg's last words to the man who aimed a gun at her in the car. A little later, her body was chucked into the Landwehr Canal, where it wasn't found until months later. 'It was as though they couldn't have her dead enough,' Roland Holst wrote appalled.

Karl Liebknecht was also murdered that same night. Just a day after the first rumors of their murders, Albert Einstein and artist Käthe Kollwitz founded the German League for Human Rights in Berlin. Many tens of thousands of people attended the memorial processions in Berlin. Commemorations were also held in other cities, including Amsterdam, where Henriette Roland Holst expressed her 'deep grief and unspeakable indignation' at the murder of her friend, whom she had 'so admired for her extraordinary gifts and heroic courage.'

As a twelve-year-old girl, Hannah Arendt was enthusiastically taken by her mother onto the streets of Königsberg on those first days of January 1919. A great admirer of Rosa Luxemburg, her mother had exclaimed: 'You must pay attention, this is a historic moment!' In Königsberg too, people had gone on mass strikes and gathered in buildings where Spartacists from Berlin had come to speak. Hannah's mother had sincerely believed that the kaiser's flight and hundreds of thousands of revolutionary socialists taking to the streets demanding the government's resignation had finally heralded a new dawn for war-ravaged Germany. But it wasn't to be.

For Hannah Arendt, the murder of the two pacifist socialists marked a historic turning point. 'Rosa Luxemburg's death became the watershed between two eras in Germany.' 'Shot on the run,' was how the police report described this premeditated murder, probably with the connivance of SPD minister Gustav Noske, who had joined the government at the end of December 1918 to ensure 'order.' It would become the standard lie in the ensuing years for the many hundreds of murders of left-wing politicians, including that of her former lover and lifelong friend Leo Jogiches. In her review of J. P. Nettl's biography Hannah Arendt wrote in the *New Yorker*: 'And since this early crime had been aided and abetted by the government, it initiated a death-dance in postwar Germany: The assassins of the extreme Right started by liquidating prominent leaders of the extreme Left— Hugo Haase and Gustav Landauer, Leo Jogiches and Eugene Leviné—and quickly moved to the center and the right-of-center—to Walter Rathenau, Matthias Erzberger, both members of the government at the time of their murder. Thus Rosa Luxemburg's death became the watershed between two eras in Germany; and it became the point of no return for the German Left.'

Captain Waldemar Pabst said unrepentantly in an interview with *Der Spiegel* in 1962 that he still believed 'that it was perfectly justifiable from a moral-theological point of view to eliminate them.' One of the other perpetrators, Lieutenant Vogel, fled to the Netherlands during the ensuing mock trial. We don't know what became of him; he may have joined the kaiser, who had also fled to the Netherlands and supported right-wing militias, and later also the Nazis, with his wife Hermine Reuss, as painstakingly reconstructed by Dutch historian Willem Pekelder in the Dutch newspaper *Trouw* in 2018. As this episode is hardly a source of national pride, most Dutch history books steer well clear of it.

Arendt argued that the murder of Luxemburg, Liebknecht, and many other socialist luminaries cleared the way for Hitler. He built his political campaign on the ruins of the First World War and the political violence that established the Weimar Republic, and soon recruited members of his paramilitary Sturmabteilung from the same Freikorps that had crushed the uprising. Hitler won the electorate over with the same anti-Semitic and anti-communist slogans that had been used against the Spartacus League. The price for this was colossal. In the ensuing decades, Luxemburg's oft-quoted phrase from the *Junius Pamphlet* was decided tragically in favor of the latter. 'Bourgeois society stands at the crossroads,' Luxemburg wrote, 'either transition to socialism or regression into barbarism.' The question Arendt pondered in her essay in *Men in Dark Times*—'Will history look different if seen through the prism of her life and work?'—must be answered in the affirmative. What would have happened to Germany if 'free socialist democracy' had succeeded can, unfortunately, only be left to our imagination.

7

The centenary of the murder of Rosa Luxemburg and Karl Liebknecht was commemorated around the world in 2019. In my hometown Amsterdam many hundreds of people came to mark the occasion at the International Institute of Social History. Interest in Hannah Arendt's work has in recent decades also grown in leaps and bounds. Although separated in history by one world war and at least two totalitarian regimes, nowadays the two women are often discussed together in articles and books, for example, German writer Simone Frieling's *Rebellinnen* (Rebels, 2018) and Canadian philosopher Diane Lamoureux's *Pensées rebelles* (Rebel Thoughts, 2010). Yet there are also important differences between the two political thinkers. Luxemburg, unencumbered by experience of the terror of totalitarian regimes, forcefully emphasized political action and activism, whereas Arendt's position was much more that of a political and philosophical spectator, as I pointed out in *The Judge & the Spectator*, a collection of essays on Hannah Arendt's political philosophy that I edited with American philosopher Dana Villa in 2000. The ambivalent relationship between thinking and acting is a recurrent motif in Arendt's work; throughout her work she tries to find a satisfactory answer to the question how philosophy and politics relate. This wasn't ever a concern for Luxemburg, who was principally a political activist. But interestingly enough, they did share some of the same ideas and convictions about freedom, human dignity, spontaneity, political commitment, and the necessity of critical and alert thinking. This chapter will consider some of the similarities in their thinking, before a closer examination of their differences, especially regarding Marxist theory.

Arendt wrote in her book *On Totalitarianism* (1951) that even after the Second World War, we should be on our guard for totalitarianism, a form of government characterized by undermining human plurality and political freedoms. Totalitarian ideologies use propaganda, fear, and violence to transform the diversity of a people into a uniform and obedient mass. They also often use scapegoat theories that appeal to the 'dangerous emotional needs of people who live in complete isolation and in fear of one another.' Totalitarianism is a political system devoted entirely to instrumentality and technocracy, with no scope for the truth or an open debating culture because everything must conform to the logic of its nationalism and xenophobia. Toward the end of her lengthy analysis, she warned that this form of government 'which as a potentiality and an ever-present danger is only too likely to stay with us from now on.'

Populist or demagogic political leaders couldn't care less about facts or fact-based truths, Arendt believed. They usually choose one idea, based on the nationalist myth of the people's 'uniqueness' and the alienness of others, to tell the same compelling story over and over. We should therefore, Arendt wrote in *The Origins of Totalitarianism*, be wary of any restriction of the freedom of expression and the dissemination of propaganda—what we nowadays call fake news—which she saw as heralding the demise of democracy. Lies, or alternative facts as they have euphemistically been dubbed, should be exposed and refuted with fact-based opinions as much as possible. For 'the ideal subject of totalitarian rule is not the convinced Nazi or the convinced Communist, but people for whom the distinction between fact and fiction . . . no longer exist[s].' In an interview with the *New York Review* shortly before her death, Arendt explained that 'if everybody always lies to you, the consequence is not that you believe the lies, but rather that nobody believes anything any longer. . . . A people that no longer can believe anything cannot make up its mind. It is deprived not only of its capacity to act but also of its capacity to think and to judge. And with such a people you can then do what you please.'

'Post-truth' was chosen as Oxford Dictionaries 2016 Word of the Year. The word may be new, but Arendt had already shown that lies or post-truths are tools favored by totalitarian regimes. Post-truth politics is a way of doing politics that is no longer concerned with facts or truths but above all with repeating emotionally charged claims. Factual objections are shrugged off or simply dismissed as irrelevant. The 2016 American elections and the Brexit referendum brought into sharp focus how much the difference between truth-based facts and lies has in many cases become merely a matter of preference. This was immortalized during the Brexit debate by Justice Secretary Gove's dismissal of economic objections to Brexit: 'People have had enough of experts.' The collapse of the distinction between truth and lies recalls the lines in George Orwell's novel *1984* that were often quoted the day after the American election: 'Everything faded into the mist. The past was erased, the erasure forgotten, the lie became truth.'

Obstructing press freedom is another tried-and-tested

tool of dictatorial regimes. 'The moment we no longer have a free press,' Arendt warned 'anything can happen.' The press in the 'free' Western world has in recent years also been subject to censorship. Former president Trump's erstwhile strategist Steve Bannon brazenly told the *New York Times* that the media should 'keep its mouth shut and just listen for a while.' Trump deliberately fomented an atmosphere of paranoia and confusion, but the press seemed to lack any adequate response to his post-truth politics. David Remnick, editor-in-chief of the *New Yorker* and an early Trump critic, argued it was because they lack the words to describe these 'post-truths,' which aren't language, just linguistic nonsense. Freedom of expression is also vulnerable in Hong Kong, eastern Europe, and India, not to mention North Korea and the Arab states; lies are told by political leaders all around the world. How often are facts distorted or obscured or blatant lies told? Whipping up a cloud of opacity, turning things around, obdurate denial, and causing endless confusion and doubt are the classical tools of a liar; unfortunately, many politicians are only too happy to turn them to account. Lying or cheating political leaders foster aversion to political governance, and history teaches us that this is a perilous development. It makes people turn their backs on politics, raising the specter of the worldlessness Arendt wrote about, which has often proved a breeding ground for barbarism and dictatorial rule. What we mustn't forget is to remain vigilant for new totalitarian tendencies in our society, Arendt points out: 'Totalitarian solutions may well survive the fall of totalitarian regimes in the form of strong temptations which will come up whenever it seems impossible to alleviate political, social, or economic misery in a manner worthy of man.'

'The public life of countries with limited freedom is so

poverty-stricken, so miserable, so rigid, so unfruitful,' Luxemburg wrote in the same vein, 'precisely because, through the exclusion of democracy, it cuts off the living sources of all spiritual riches and progress.' Hence her sharp criticism of Lenin and Trotsky, who, from the start of the Russian Revolution in 1917, restricted democratic rights to free speech, dissolved parliament, failed to call free elections, and established a one-party system. As with Arendt, freedom of expression and political association were inviolable democratic values for Luxemburg, not to be subverted by any ideology. 'It is a well-known and indisputable fact that without a free and untrammeled press, without the unlimited right of association and assemblage, the rule of the broad masses of the people is entirely unthinkable,' Luxemburg wrote.

The Russian Revolution had nothing to do with a real socialist democracy for her: 'Without general elections, without unrestricted freedom of press and assembly, without a free struggle of opinion, life dies out in every public institution, becomes a mere semblance of life, in which only the bureaucracy remains as the active element. Public life gradually falls asleep, a few dozen party leaders of inexhaustible energy and boundless experience direct and rule . . . such conditions must inevitably cause a brutalization of public life: attempted assassinations, shooting of hostages, etc.' She predicted the revolution would result in a dictatorship by a few leaders, with the promise of freedom and equality soon breached, swiftly followed by terror. 'Freedom only for the supporters of the government, only for the members of one party—however numerous they may be—is no freedom at all,' she wrote. 'Freedom is always and exclusively freedom for the one who thinks differently.'

Arendt concurred, dryly asking in her essay on Luxemburg, 'And haven't events proved her right?' Freedom wasn't something to be trifled with for either of them. It's the prerequisite for every political change. Both women also emphasized that this freedom can only be acquired 'in concert' with others: that is, together with others, when private interests are set aside for the public good—*de res publica*. This can take place in public but also at home around the kitchen table, if a conversation shows *amor mundi*, love of the world. Hannah Arendt was fond of quoting poet René Char's famous lines:

> At every meal that we eat together,
> Freedom is invited to sit down.
> The chair remains vacant but the place is set.

Rosa Luxemburg and Hannah Arendt were critical mavericks, unafraid of engaging in controversy and putting forward opinions which affronted their intellectual supporters. Sharpening critical consciousness and encouraging people to form their own judgment or opinion and share it publicly—in words, writing, or action—was the core of both thinkers' work. 'One deed, and sometimes one word, suffices to change every constellation,' Arendt wrote in *The Human Condition*. She admired Socrates's philosophical method. Seeing himself as the 'gadfly' of Athens, he used his idiosyncratic and controversial opinions to consciously sting Athenians out of their intellectual torpor and into thinking for themselves.

The Socratic method is also known as 'maieutics'—literally midwifery—and it's tempting to call Luxemburg and

Arendt 'midwives' of modern political philosophy for their similarities to the Greek philosopher. They, too, considered it their task to help others bring forth their critical thoughts, as they are all that can clear the path for new beginnings: 'The life span of man running toward death would inevitably carry everything human to ruin and destruction,' Arendt wrote in *The Human Condition*, 'if it were not for the capacity of interrupting it and beginning something new, a faculty which is inherent in action like an ever-present reminder that men, although they must die, are not born in order to die but in order to begin.'

They were engaged in reclaiming political space for freedom, necessary for making new beginnings of this kind, as Sidonia Blättler, Irene M. Marti, and Senem Saner show in their essay 'Rosa Luxemburg and Hannah Arendt: Against the Destruction of Political Spheres of Freedom' (2005). They wanted to protect this political sphere of freedom from domination by economic powers. For Arendt, modern consumer society meant the loss of community spirit, namely the political spirit of shared responsibility for the world; she believed it resulted in people becoming desolate, alienated, and rootless. Although she didn't use the word 'capitalism' very often in her later work, her criticism of mass consumer society is in many ways similar to Luxemburg's critique of capitalist society; one could even ask whether there is really any difference.

What's clear to both Arendt and Luxemburg is that a consumerist, capitalist society is incapable of taking care of the world and the people inhabiting it. As Arendt wrote in *The Crisis of Culture*, it is based on the principle of immediate consumption and economic profit rather than any sustainable care. As our society nowadays is largely characterized by consumerism and capitalist benefits, our concern for the world is more pressing than ever. Luxemburg and Arendt didn't just criticize this type of society, they also came up with concrete proposals for other democratic models, which could increase freedom, critical thinking, and political involvement.

Before considering some of Luxemburg's and Arendt's political 'advice' for renewing and 'democratizing' democracy, it is instructive to look first more closely at the main differences between their political convictions to reach that goal. To get a clearer impression of the differences between their views of social democratic society, the following chapter is an excerpt from a fictive dialogue I recently wrote for a Belgian theater company. Luxemburg and Arendt meet in a nondescript waiting room—a transit lounge between worlds, so to speak—where their discussion sometimes develops into rather heated and passionate debate. We will of course never know how conversation between these two giants of twentieth-century political history would have gone, but we can be certain of one crucial element: Marx's shadow would have loomed large over almost every imaginable subject.

8

The Prospect of Revolution

A FICTITIOUS DIALOGUE BETWEEN
HANNAH ARENDT AND ROSA LUXEMBURG

On December 4, 1975, Hannah Arendt died unexpectedly during a dinner at her apartment in New York. Some unspecified time later, she walks into a room with a simple bunkbed, a few chairs, and a table, where a woman is seated and writing intently. She doesn't at first notice her guest.

H: Excuse me, but . . . ?

R: Oh, you gave me a fright!

H: But is this where we . . . end up?

R: You could say that, yes.

H: Really? I'd imagined something rather different.

R: I don't believe you did.

H: No, you're right—I hadn't honestly imagined anything.

R: In that case, the now isn't that bad.

H: I've been traveling for so long that I'm glad to arrive somewhere at least.

R: Once a refugee, always a refugee . . .

H: You too?

R: Yes, though a little earlier on Chronos's line. Not much, just a flash in eternity. And I didn't come walking like you; I was sitting on a farmer's cart. Fleeing the tsar's Polish vassals, who were hanging all the members of the revolutionary party in

Warsaw. I decided not to wait around for that. I arrived safe and sound in Zurich.

H: Frau Luxemburg. Is that you?

R: It certainly is.

H: What a surprise! Pleased to meet you! I'm Hannah Arendt.

R: I know, Frau Arendt, welcome. You've also been to Switzerland, haven't you? I loved Zurich in those years: all the world's idealist outcasts dreamed together in that wonderful city on the banks of Lake Zurich. The only place in Europe where both sexes were admitted to university.

H: This place also feels a bit like a Swiss guesthouse, don't you think? We ended up in Geneva when we fled Germany. I especially remember the geraniums on the balconies, and the clear, soft, sparkling water in Lake Geneva . . .

R: Oh, yes! And the wonder after the long railway tunnel, when you suddenly find yourself gliding above the immense blue mirror of the lake, with all the tiny steamboats leaving a long veil of white foam behind them.

H: And all of it capped by the blinding white peaks of the Dents du Midi!

R: Come and sit down; I'll pour you a cup of tea. You can have the top bunk—unfortunately, I can't get up there with my gammy leg. I'd love to gaze at the stars from my bed. They extend all the way across to that window, like white jasmine flowers clambering up the window frame.

H: Fancy meeting here, Frau Luxemburg. What a coincidence.

R: Coincidence is God's way of remaining anonymous.

H: You can say that again. You must know, I greatly admire your work. I wrote a long piece about it in the *New Yorker* in the 1960s.

R: A good article, yes.

H: Have you read it?

R: We know everything we want to here. It was also a little more comprehensive than the few sentences you devoted to me in the rest of your work. Tea?

H: Please—but . . . I regularly referred to your work, didn't I?

R: Do you take sugar? A splash of milk? Some people find Russian tea too strong.

H: No, thanks. I take my tea black. With sweetener, please.

R: Black with a spoonful of America. Why aren't I surprised?

H: I beg your pardon?

R: How did it go again? 'In the following chapters Karl Marx will be criticized.'

H: Oh, *The Human Condition,* one of my first books. I thought Marx was too fixated on the human condition of work and labor and paid too little attention to the human condition of action and contemplation.

R: A fine trichotomy, for sure, but unfortunately not a voluntary choice for most people.

H: You don't beat about the bush!

R: I'm delighted finally to be able to speak to you!

H: So am I.

R: [Pensively] Perhaps you see us too much from a philosophical perspective.

H: That's impossible—I'm not a philosopher.

R: If *you* aren't a philosopher then who is?

H: I might have studied philosophy, but I didn't remain one. I took leave of philosophy because I thought it was too hostile and indifferent toward everything that had anything to do with politics. And we've seen what that leads to.

R: Come off it! You're one of the most important philosophers of the twentieth century.

H: My profession, inasmuch as you can speak of one, is political theory. I want to breathe new life into the political domain by saving it from the clutches of economism and technocracy. And I'm of the opinion that Marx paid too little heed to this free political space, with his focus on things like work and money.

R: Karl was originally a legal scholar. He grew up in Trier, a poor wine-growing region, where Saint-Simon's and Fourier's ideas really struck a chord. They were the ones who inspired Marx in his struggle for social-economic justice. He believed that political thinkers had to be actively engaged in the world. 'The philosophers have only interpreted the world, in various ways . . .'

H: '. . . The point is to change it.' Yes, of course, we know that quotation, but the question is still: in which direction? I think Marx made politics too much of an economic question. I don't believe that work is humans' most important activity. People are so much more than an economic cog in a giant production system.

R: Most of us simply have to work to keep our heads above water.

H: You are saying the same thing—work is a necessary evil.

R: It gives some people a sense of fulfilment.

H: But for most people it's a necessity for survival.

R: All the more reason to organize it well and fairly.

H: That goes without saying! But then we need to focus on what touches people most profoundly, like freedom of thought, action, expression, and creation.

R: So, work doesn't set you free?

H: That they placed that slogan at the entrances to the concentration camps shows its grotesque cynicism. Working to survive makes you unfree because necessity is the opposite of freedom. Only unpaid work sets you free, provided it's done voluntarily.

R: Unpaid labor? Nowadays many people need several jobs to get by.

H: Would you mind if I smoked?

R: Go ahead. Another cup of tea?

H: Could I have something stronger? Do you fancy some Four Roses? Besides, it must be the end of the afternoon by now.

R: The clock on the mantlepiece has no power here.

H: That's good news! I've got another bottle in my suitcase. I propose a toast. To this encounter! With a Kentucky straight bourbon. Wonderful. Cheers!

R: May I ask you something you might find less wonderful? Has it ever struck you how you criticized capitalism less and less once you emigrated to America?

H: What makes you say that? I've written in the most critical terms about Western consumer society.

R: Certainly, and also about the stultifying 'consumptive attitude,' as you so succinctly put it, and the general commercialization of society, which is liable to consume everything it touches and is incapable of dealing with anything sustainably. But you seem to have gradually lost sight of the most important thing—the cause of all of it!

H: What do you mean?

R: It's not people's voluntary choice to live like that. They don't just wake up one day and think: 'You know what, I'm going to take on three jobs at the same time and pursue unquenchable consumerism!'

H: That consumptive attitude is caused by large-scale industrialization and the submergence of the political domain.

R: But that's not the whole story! This 'attitude' is also hammered into people by politics, industry, advertising, and culture. People are subordinated to the capitalist myth of growth and un-restrained consumption which exhausts both them and na-ture, while only profiting big business. This inequality is partly the result of the fact that capital and the means of pro-duction are owned by a small minority, while the vast major-ity has to work for meager wages.

H: I engaged with Marx's ideas for years; I even wanted to write a book on the subject—but unfortunately never got round to it.

R: I'd really have been interested in what you had to say.

H: I wanted to show that the amalgamation of Marx's political and state-led economic policy has a Western counterpart. Not only thanks to the focus on work and money but the amalga-mation of politics and economy too.

R: You can't be serious!

H: In the sense that neither guarantees a free political space, which isn't sullied by economic interests. On top of which, other issues also demanded my attention—Eichmann, who was arrested in Argentina, and covering his trial in Jerusa-lem for the *New Yorker*. All of us were forced to revisit the hor-rors of the Holocaust. It was exhausting—as were the resulting controversies. I couldn't devote all my time to Marx.

R: I know. And you took an exceptionally courageous position.

H: I lost good friends, who couldn't understand why I didn't con-sider Eichmann a satanic monster but rather a cowardly, cal-lous administrator. Evil doesn't have an easily recognizable di-abolic face; no, it isn't that simple. Evil has the undistinguished face of people who are too afraid or lazy to ask critical ques-tions or reflect on their own actions. That's what I mean by the banality of evil—not that it's meaningless but unthinking.

R: Perhaps the term was a little impolitic?

H: It expresses exactly what I mean. Evil isn't deep or profound; it spreads swiftly and in a superficial way across the populace when the circumstances are favorable enough—by which I mean that political rulers foster inequality, instill fear, propound false myths about the superiority of a race, and muzzle journalists, academics, and artists.

R: Having to look day after day at that man in that glass booth can't have been easy.

H: I observed him for weeks, longer than was good for me—because his banality was insufferable. He just sat there cleaning his glasses during the trial, as if that would help focus his conscience again. A mediocre little man, lacking talent or courage, who only spoke in hackneyed clichés but was responsible for the deportation of millions of Jews. How could I help but sometimes bursting into laughter?

R: You were obliged to watch an absurd performance, with a buffoon playing the mass murderer.

H: I kept asking myself: how on earth was it possible that almost the entire German population—doctors, teachers, workers, lawyers, nurses, professors—didn't rebel?

R: And you came up with answers—arguing that totalitarian regimes eventually manage to subdue the population with a false ideology and institutionalized terror. How they use fear, violence, and indoctrination to transform them into a docile mass, in which individuals' voices no longer count and critical thinking and imagination have been eliminated.

H: I tried to understand all of it.

R: Oh, you did more than that. Your understanding is a warning to all of us. Every single day. You showed that there's always a threat of racial hatred, intolerance, and the abuse of power—near our homes and maybe even in them—which is why we must be vigilant. You should know that I'm also a great admirer of your work, oh my goodness, from your very first book, about Rahel Varnhagen, to *The Life of the Mind*.

H: Thank you. Kind of you to say so.

R: There's still that one issue, though—your position on Marxist theory. You must have discussed it often enough, back then in Berlin. With your first husband Gunther Anders, with his cousin Walter Benjamin, and later with Heinrich Blücher, your second husband, who fought to the bitter end on our side and became a member of the German Communist Party. He's the link between us, do you see?

H: My husband hasn't been a member of the KPD since 1928 because of Stalin!

R: I'd like to discuss Marx and his ideas—and not dictators like Stalin. You surely know that I denounced Lenin and Trotsky as early as 1917 for the total lack of democracy in the second Russian Revolution.

H: Certainly, you were one of the first to do so. Shall we have some more whiskey?

R: Go ahead. Our conversation is already giving me rosy cheeks! I opposed Lenin's abolition of the multiparty system and his restriction of democratic freedoms because freedom is always and exclusively freedom for the one who thinks differently. I wrote that—against Lenin and his destruction of the political domain. Heaven only knows what I'd have written about his mustachioed successor if I had been granted more time.

H: Lenin, Trotsky, Stalin, Castro—not a single leader has established a socialist utopia without violence and oppression. And no one can sincerely call themselves a Marxist since Stalin's pact with Hitler in 1939.

R: But how can you denounce someone's ideas on the grounds of crimes committed by his supposed successors? Marx's ideas about socioeconomic injustice have nothing to do with Stalin. And please let's not forget that no country has established a capitalist utopia without large-scale violence and injustice.

H: That's also true. Cheers.

R: Do you know, it sometimes saddens me that Marx—and so all of us who strove for democratic socialism—is again and again the target of recriminations about Stalin's crimes. What's the reason for this incredible anachronism? We're dismissed as 'Stalinists' while we were long dead before that failed priest rose to power. Even you blame me for Stalin. While he had hardly read a line of Marx's work! Lust for power and sexual drive typify the man. And making everyone bow and scrape before him to compensate for his alcoholic father's beatings!

H: Lenin helped him come to power.

R: But what does that have to do with us? We were engaged in a political struggle against social injustice. As was your mother. We'd hoped that the October Revolution wouldn't only be the end of the tsarist regime but would finally usher in a democratic, socialist regime.

H: Yes, she was wrong too.

R: It was not to be—the timing wasn't right. To my mind, it was actually completely wrong, but we could no longer stop the uprising. A popular uprising always starts unexpectedly, we can't determine the timing. And that wasn't a good moment. The people were too exhausted and defeated after four years of war for any kind of revolution. Anyway, you know your history. But what I don't understand is that you didn't defend our ideas more. That you even had the temerity to claim that capitalism and socialism are twins? Just wearing a different hat? I'm sorry, but that's utter nonsense!

H: Because Marx too wanted to subordinate the political to the economic domain. And that's a serious error! To genuinely act and judge freely we must keep the political space free from economic necessities. This includes expropriation of the means of production, which Marx advocated, because that is a political intervention in the economic domain—which is treading on thin ice. Because a process of expropriation can't be organized peacefully, and you're riding on a tiger's back: you can no longer get off—the process becomes unstoppable. We learned as much from the Soviet Union. Marxist expropriation and capitalist overexploitation are the same to me in this sense—they destroy the political domain and deprive people of their freedom.

R: I really don't understand how you can equate capitalism with socialism.

H: What they share is subordination of the political to the economic domain. And this is lethal to political freedom and plurality, which can only take shape in the political domain. This results in a kind of mass people, whether communist or capitalist—people who lack individual uniqueness and only pursue their own self-interest, instead of the public good. You can only start anew both verbally and physically when you're free of necessities—which I call natality. People can interrupt the course of things by taking a new initiative, but this requires the freedom of the political and cultural world. This isn't possible in an order dominated by money and primary gratification.

R: That sounds high-minded, but the problem is your way of thinking is incapable of thwarting the destruction wreaked by hypercapitalism.

H: The only way of doing so is by separating the economic and political domains and fundamentally renewing democracy.

R: The other problem with your thinking is its presumption of equality, while unfortunately it doesn't exist. Many groups aren't even represented in politics and are in no position to indulge in your freedom. If you have to work for a few dollars a day you don't get around to critical thinking! Because you're exhausted. My question is: why is such a vast number of people exhausted, while a relatively small group of people live in ever-greater luxury and extravagance? How can we put this right?

H: Didn't Marx say that that would take care of itself? The class struggle between the bourgeoise and the proletariat would inevitably be won by the workers, wouldn't it? Not that we've seen much evidence for this; quite frankly, I never believed in that dialectical myth. The bourgeoisie will always fight tooth and nail to retain its privileges. The free market will eventually get its hands on everything, and everything will be merely a question of money—then there really won't be any possibility of change.

R: I too have often contended that the dialectic dynamic wouldn't operate unaided. It'll only work if we inaugurate another political model, which isn't only just but enables more freedom and development for everyone. That's why we strove for a council democracy, which would put an end to the incestuous collaboration between government and industry.

H: I also consider popular councils of this kind an essential supplement to parliamentary democracy, which inherently contains oligarchic features. It's about involving far more than a few hundred parliamentarians in discussions about the world and them learning to judge and act for themselves. In my opinion, Marx had too little appreciation of the possibility of democratic renewal; instead he kept beating the drum of class struggle and expropriation as the ultimate means of fostering the dialectic process. I don't believe this, and that's why I consider political freedoms more important than economic freedoms, which stem automatically from political freedom. Take the Paris Commune in 1871. The Parisian populace used democratic means to institute a form of self-government, which greatly improved the living conditions of the lower classes.

R: I'm as great an admirer of the Paris Commune as you, but you too know how it was bloodily suppressed by French rulers a few months later. So, the question is how this can be averted next time, and whether this requires revolutionary forces. Revolution is perhaps the only answer to the immense conflict between our modern ideals of justice and equality and the bitter and cruel consequences of capitalism. Also, not every revolution has to be accompanied by bloodshed.

H: Unfortunately, history isn't on your side. Recall the words of eighteenth-century French revolutionary Pierre Vergniaud: 'So, citizens, it must be feared that the Revolution, like Saturn, successively devours its children.' This very socially and politically engaged lawyer ended up on the guillotine himself. And isn't this what happened to you and other members of the Spartacus League?

R: Things could have gone differently if we'd been able to choose our moment, if there hadn't been four years of world war and we hadn't been betrayed.

H: Revolution eats its children, and the proletariat's peaceful dialectic victory has proven to be a chimera. We're left with no choice but to fundamentally renew the democratic order so that people make better use of their political freedom and undertake new initiatives. Popular councils could very well be a first step along this path.

R: But then we must first ensure that their 'needs' are met so that they have the necessary time and energy. You can't say to people who are homeless or starving, 'Listen, we're not going to intervene economically; we're only going to pursue political renewal.' You have to do both at the same time. That's why I advocate a cooperative economy, in which production is no longer focused on enriching the few but on meeting the community's needs. An economy which fosters local production and wisely utilizes land, goods, and labor. This economy aims to give everyone a dignified life and is as concerned with workers' moral health as with their physical health. *That* is politics!

H: I have no idea how you'd organize this in the context of global power politics.

R: You just have to make a start! Popular councils can help get a local, co-operative economy up and running. Everyone is invited every so often to sit on them and help decide important issues. Only then will people feel heard.

H: Popular councils can certainly increase political freedom and involvement—as well as community spirit. But I don't think they'll make people more receptive to expropriation of their homes.

R: Only big business will lose out—it goes without saying that the people can keep their homes, workshops, farms, and studios. But big business will finally have to repay its debt to society. And the means of production will be cooperatively owned by local communities. So that the people will no longer be expropriated for the profits and share options of the few. Only then will people again engage with politics. As Bertold Brecht wrote, even though he undoubtedly meant it cynically, 'First comes food then morality.'

H: How can we ever achieve this as separate states? It'd require a world revolution.

R: The nation-state, like nationalism, is an invention of capitalist imperialism. We must found a new democratic Socialist International and reach out across borders. Just start dismantling big business by obliging them to return their profits to local communities. Pull down borders that divide people into haves and have-nots. Self-rule in the form of popular councils, which are connected to each other across borders to deal with environmental problems and injustice.

H: How are you going to defend people's rights if there are no longer borders? Who is going to protect us then? Won't we all become refugees?

R: But Frau Arendt, without borders there'll no longer be refugees! All of our fates will be connected, and we'll have to try to find a way together! On second thoughts, I'll take you up on that glass of bourbon.

H: Cheers!

9

'Before a revolution happens, it is perceived as impossible; after it happens, it is seen as inevitable' is one of the most famous quotes attributed to Rosa Luxemburg. The socialist council democracy she envisioned was chiefly inspired by the Paris Commune (1871) and aimed to allow all sections of the population to express their opinion and share in political decision-making power in 'popular councils.' In 2018 and 2019, French newspapers regularly drew comparisons between the yellow vests uprising and the French Revolution of 1789 or the student uprising of May 1968. Much less was said about the revolt a hundred years earlier, which has gone down in history as the 'Paris Commune.' This popular uprising against the French government was also prompted by spontaneous protests against poverty, unemployment, and unjust taxation. After a chaotic start, the commune organized itself effectively for several months in district and popular councils, in which women and workers participated for the first time in history.

The Communards, democratically elected by over 200,000 Parisians, successfully implemented several important reforms in a short time; the food supply was restored, tradespeople's debts were forgiven, and public facilities were reinstituted. Hannah Arendt speaks admiringly of self-governing potential of these popular councils in her book *On Revolu-tion*. Rosa Luxemburg also describes the Paris Commune as the first attempt to establish a socialist democracy, with the people given a political say. In her final text, with the bitterly ironic title "Order Prevails in Berlin," written just hours be-fore her death, she recalls—unaware of her own fate—'the bestial cruelty' and the lives of 'the poorly armed, starving Parisian proletariat and their defenseless women and chil-dren' sacrificed in the suppression of this popular uprising; 30,000 Communards were killed by the French government army in May 1871 and another 40,000 were imprisoned. It is as though Luxemburg was expressing a premonition of what was about to befall her—and many others in the first months of 1919.

The extraordinary feature of the Paris Commune is that the uprising demanded not only liberation from poverty and want but also freedom of political action in the form of 'pop-ular councils.' Arendt considers this an essential distinction, arguing in *On Revolution* that revolts only have a chance of success if they don't demand just economic 'liberation' but political freedom too. The problem with revolts which only make economic demands is that they don't fundamentally change the political model that forces people into poverty. Merely demanding adjustments in the form of higher wages leaves the political system unaffected. Liberation from pov-erty and oppression is a precondition for freedom, but it doesn't automatically lead to political freedom, which for Arendt always means establishing something new.

In the same book, she describes the emergence of self-governing councils, like those in the Russian Revolution of 1905 and the Hungarian Revolution in 1956, as the political manifestation of this kind of renewal. She speaks hopefully of these councils as 'oases in a desert,' allowing citizens to participate in political action. The problem with the representative system is that it 'can be called oligarchic in the sense that public happiness and public freedom have again become the privilege of the few'; 'only the representatives of the people, not the people themselves, [have] an opportunity to engage in those activities of "expressing, discussing and deciding" which in a positive sense are the activities of freedom.' As for the rest of the population, 'the most the citizen can hope for is to be "represented," whereby it is obvious that the only thing which can be represented and delegated is interest, or the welfare of the constituents, but neither their actions nor their opinions. In this system the opinions of the people are indeed unascertainable for the simple reason that they are non-existent.' As we have seen, one of the main reasons for the institutional crisis in France is that the yellow vests no longer feel politically represented at all since the election of Macron and his neoliberal La République En Marche! party.

'It would be tempting to spin out further the potentialities of the councils,' Arendt wrote, 'but it certainly is wiser to say with Jefferson, "begin them only for a single purpose; they will soon show for what others they are the best instruments".' I think the time has come for us to actually get started with this. One of the demands of the gilets jaunes was the introduction of citizens' initiative referendums to increase political freedom and involvement. Instead of everyone ticking a box at a referendum and hoping for the best, we could set up specially elected citizens' councils, giving members the time—and financial compensation—to properly examine a subject and cast a vote together. This would increase popular political involvement, as well as promote a sense of community, and significantly diminish the impression of 'not being heard or represented.'

Likewise, these citizens' councils might just take the wind out of the sails of right-wing extremists because they would give people a place in the world, perhaps making them feel less powerless and displaced. Restoring people's autonomy and responsibility will make the world flourish. Rosa Luxemburg and Hannah Arendt fervently advocated this form of direct democracy in their work, as do contemporary authors like Belgian writer David van Reybrouck. In his book *Tegen de verkiezingen* (Against Elections, 2014), he condemns the failure of parliamentary democracy and citizens' waning faith in democracy. In a variation of the jury model, he proposes choosing citizens by lot to discuss political issues together. The idea of selection by lot might at first sound outlandish, but as Bernard Manin points out in *The Principles of Representative Government*, it is a very old one. In fact, for the ancient Greeks, 'lot is described as *the* democratic selection method, while election is seen as more oligarchic or aristocratic.' This mechanism was used in classical Athenian democracy to appoint the vast majority of magistrates. Only posts requiring specific competencies, such as generals, were selected by election. Lot has the advantage of properly reflecting the population and is unencumbered by party politics or electoral interests.

For several years, I took part in a 'citizen council' in Amsterdam, consisting of about twenty local residents from various cultural backgrounds. The initiative was intended to promote social cohesion in my neighborhood, which was certainly called for because we didn't so much live together as lead parallel lives. Our meetings were instructive and inspiring, and they succeeded not only in terms of the projects we developed but also in their objective as a multicultural neighborhood council. During our long conversations, we got to know each other's stories, points of view, and backgrounds; took various initiatives; and so engaged in political action together. We crossed various national, religious, and cultural boundaries, putting into practice the plurality Hannah Arendt had advocated, which she saw as the cornerstone of democracy, as well as our ability 'to think with an enlarged mentality.' I not only understood the philosophy and cultural views of my neighbors much better but felt as though my soul, or the innermost core of my humanity, was expanded by these meetings.

Both Luxemburg and Arendt point out that the political and cultural world, which lies between people, isn't a self-evidently 'human' world. Arendt contends that the world only becomes human when it is the object of our attention, involvement, and conversation. When we turn away from the public world out of frustration, lack of time, or indifference, we risk a form of worldlessness, which can lead to barbarism. Rosa Luxemburg goes further than Arendt in denouncing capitalist society more radically, arguing that it is based on the fundamental misapprehension that a just world can be created on the basis of competition, contest, and exploitation of others. But both political thinkers call for political freedom, social and economic justice, and political involvement as the only things that can guarantee democracy in a society. Of course, Luxemburg's call to win over the masses and give voice to our protest in a more radical way was louder: 'To be a human being means to joyfully toss your entire life "on the giant scales of fate" if it must be so,' Luxemburg wrote in a letter to Mathilda Wurm in 1916, 'and at the same time to rejoice in the brightness of every day and the beauty of every cloud.' But they were, in my opinion, both like modern Antigones, defending the right to resist when legislation or political governance couldn't be reconciled with conscience—that is, the ability to distinguish between good and evil. 'Antigone' literally means counter-movement; democracy needs opposition and opposition movements to remain healthy and dynamic.

In her essay "Civil Disobedience" (1970), Hannah Arendt welcomed as enthusiastically as Luxemburg the possibilities offered by political resistance, be it demonstrations, strikes, conscientious objection, or other forms. The essay was prompted by the increasing number of Americans refusing to participate in the Vietnam War or comply with racist laws, such as segregation in public transport. Arendt greatly valued this kind of civil disobedience: 'Civil disobedients are nothing but the latest form of voluntary association, and that they are thus quite in tune with the oldest traditions of the country.' If particular laws or political policies conflict with our conscience, then it is our 'civic duty' to do something about them. Arendt believed that civil disobedience could be an important 'remedy for the failure of institutions, the unreliability of men, and the uncertain nature of the future.' She also once noted that 'political questions are far too serious to be left to the politicians.'

10

Autumn came to an end, but the French yellow vests kept going. Returning to the Netherlands, we couldn't have guessed that they would carry on for more than another year. We now know that not only were thousands of people arrested but people also died. Many thousands of demonstrators were wounded as well, including several journalists, losing an eye or a hand after being hit by rubber bullets fired by the French police. David Dufresne's powerful 2020 documentary, *The Monopoly of Violence*, calls into question the legitimacy of the French state's use of excessive violence and police brutality in France.

Apart from using violence, the French government tried to pacify the uprising by canceling the fuel tax rise and increasing the minimum wage, but it was too little too late. As the conflict dragged on, public support for the uprising dropped a bit but was still considerable, despite all the casualties and months of inconvenience thanks to traffic jams; the demonstrators still represented a large majority in spring 2019. The same couldn't be said of the Assemblée nationale, the French parliament, where just 18 percent of parliamentarians supported the protest movement. This dramatic contrast makes painfully clear that this popular uprising stemmed partly from a lack of political representation. Most protesters didn't feel at all represented by Macron's new party La République En Marche!, most of whose members are highly educated or from the upper classes. En Marche! more or less wiped the Parti socialiste off the map in the last elections, leaving many people feeling completely unrepresented.

The Covid-19 pandemic stifled the French revolt—as well as uprisings elsewhere—but it doesn't mark an end to the institutional crisis, either in France or other Western countries. Brexit and the 2020 American elections laid bare a profound crisis in both Britain and the United States. And the last few years have been far from tranquil in other Western countries. In 2019, there were large-scale demonstrations in Hungary, Germany, and Serbia, and a veritable school student revolt against climate change started in Sweden, rapidly spreading across Europe and then practically everywhere. American protests against racism and police violence won't be thwarted by a virus or Trump's rabble-rousing rhetoric since George Floyd's murder, although communal tensions will probably be further enflamed. The result of this struggle against racism is still very unclear, but it will be greatly influenced by the attitude, actions, and tone of the American government and the new president Joe Biden and his vice president Kamala Harris.

All around the world we see the rise of movements opposing neoliberal governments, which have, over the course over the past few decades, benefited the private sector, the rich, and the multinationals at the expense of the poor, the environment, and the public sector; these injustices will certainly have repercussions. There are also serious concerns in many Western countries about the demise of the democratic rule of law and the freedom of expression. At a certain point, we will all have to take a stand, raise our voices, and join the public debate. The question is of course: how are we going to turn the tide? Figuratively, turning the tide means intervening to stop or change the direction of an inevitable course of events. It's a popular expression—beloved of politicians the world over—because carrying on down the same path looks undesirable, or even fatal. What many people don't seem to realize is that actually doing so requires almost superhuman effort. It sometimes sounds like people are talking about flipping a seashell rather than turning the tide, the imperturbable and irresistible force governing the rise and fall of sea levels. But perhaps the seeming impossibility of the effort is what speaks to the imagination. 'Be realistic—demand the impossible' was one of the slogans daubed on Parisian walls, quaysides, and bridges during the French uprising in May 1968. This revolt was characterized by *le pouvoir de dire non*—the power to say no—as French thinkers like Albert Camus and Simone Weil called it, clearing the path for a 'new sensibility' in which change could take place.

I think many people now agree that the tide of looming economic, political, and ecological crisis must be turned, but fewer of us seem inspired to really set out on the new political course implied. People want to get straight down to business, as it were, with practical proposals to be applied in existing structures, and then are surprised when confronted with resistance to radical transitions. Every uprising or revolution has both an unexpected as well as an 'impossible' or 'utopian' aspect—literally: a good but as yet nonexistent place—which first shakes up and expands the spirit, allowing it to set out a new course and resist. Therefore, we also need 'utopian' stories, ideas, and prospects to get us going; popular councils are probably one of these utopian prospects, but they nevertheless fulfill a very real urgency.

The French gilets jaunes didn't know they were sparking off a popular uprising, now dubbed a *révolution des citoyens*, let alone that they had a program for the subsequent period. No one yet knows whether the seventy consecutive Saturdays of protests had much effect—in the Netherlands, we look on with our conventional Dutch skepticism—but they have in any case illuminated the possibility of protest and therefore the freedom of political action, which is hopeful in itself and even something of a relief. We know we need a fundamental change of course if we want to keep the earth livable and the world humane. We know we have to turn the tide of society toward a politics of sustainability and solidarity. Reforming public affairs requires more than just pinning our hopes on future victories; we must also seek inspiration in the stories of political thinkers from the past. They can help us better prepare for the momentum, which I called the kairotic moment of change in my book *Kairos: Een nieuwe bevlogenheid* (Kairos: A New Engagement, 2014), when the unexpected opportunity to turn the tide suddenly arises.

'There is nothing more changeable than human psychology,' Rosa Luxemburg wrote in a letter to Mathilde Wurm. 'That's especially because the psyche of the masses, like Thalatta, [*sic*] the eternal sea, always bears within it every latent possibility: deathly stillness and raging storm, the basest cowardice and the wildest heroism. The masses are always what they must be according to the circumstances of the times, and they are always on the verge of becoming something totally different from what they seem to be.' Let's hope that we'll be able to go all out together, turn the tide, and foster a society based on sustainability, solidarity, and inclusivity. We don't actually have much choice; business as usual isn't an option.

Rosa Luxemburg and Hannah Arendt were both driven by a political struggle for freedom, and love and responsibility for the world. 'I've begun so late, really only in recent years, to truly love the world,' Hannah Arendt wrote to philosopher Karl Jaspers in 1955. 'Out of gratitude I want to call my book on political theories "Amor Mundi."' The book was given another title, *The Human Condition*, but 'love for the world' was a recurring subject in her work. It's understandable that Arendt—who fled the Nazis as a young philosopher in the late 1930s—needed time to learn to love the world again. Subjecting the world to meticulous and critical examination undoubtedly demanded great courage. This makes it even more remarkable that she so emphatically advanced *amor mundi* in her work as a remedy to the peril of *Weltlosigkeit*—worldlessness—and the ensuing violence of totalitarian regimes. 'We humanize what is going on in the world and in ourselves,' Arendt wrote in *Men in Dark Times*, 'only by speaking of it, and in the course of speaking of it we learn to be human.'

Arendt repeatedly emphasizes that establishing a common world with others, where speaking and judging are the most important activities in which 'sharing-the-world-with-others comes to pass,' is also the political function of philosophers, who must 'help to establish a kind of common world,' as she writes in *Philosophy and Politics*. Socrates was her famous example of philosopher of this kind whose thinking wasn't opposed to politics but was itself a matter of moving amongst others in the world and exploring their opinions. In *Lectures on Kant's Political Philosophy,* she writes, 'Socrates's uniqueness lies in this concentration on thinking itself, regardless of results. What he actually did was to make public, in discourse, the thinking process.'

This 'making public' of the thinking process is an anti-authoritarian way of thinking, she continues, that 'exposes itself to "the test of free and open examination," and this means that the more people participate in it, the better.' As I described in more detail with Dana Villa in *The Judge & the Spectator*, for Arendt critical thinking means not only applying critical standards to one's own thought but also comparing it to the possible judgments of others. Thinking with an 'enlarged mentality,' as she describes in her Kant Lectures: 'To think with an enlarged mentality means that one trains one's imagination to go visiting.'

Hannah Arendt and Rosa Luxemburg both believed that critical thinking and 'sharing the world with others' are a crucial counterbalance to *amor sui*, the egotism preeminent in capitalism. In her Kant Lectures Arendt notes that a valuable judgment can only be the result of 'disregarding its subjective private conditions' because 'private conditions condition us.' Imagination, reflection, and thinking with an enlarged mentality 'enable us to liberate ourselves from' these private interests and conditions. We have to transcend our egocentrism and individual interests and become 'impartial' by representing the perspectives of others who are absent. This is what Arendt called 'thinking in my own identity where actually I am not.' Disinterestedness is in this sense an important characteristic of the Arendtian critical thinking subject.

Going beyond the domain of physical survival and private interests and focusing on the political and cultural world which binds us doesn't just liberate us but makes us finally *mensch*—human, as Luxemburg would say. Without this world, we lack what largely determines our hope, freedom, and humanity: our inclusive capacity to put ourselves in someone else's place and the creative capacity to make a new beginning. In 2004 Adrienne Rich wrote in the preface to *The Rosa Luxemburg Reader* that we can learn from Luxemburg how the injustice and violence of a society pervaded by capitalism endures nowadays. 'Rosa Luxemburg travels into the twenty-first century like a great messenger bird, spanning continents, scanning history, to remind us that our present is not new but a continuation of a long human conflict changing only in intensity and scope. Her fiery critical intellect and ardent spirit are as vital for this time as in her own.' And thanks to Luxemburg's analyses we are fully conscious that casting a vote every couple of years isn't enough to fulfil our political freedom. Finally, we can find inspiration in her letters: 'to be a human being,' she wrote, 'is the main thing, above all else. And that means: to be firm and clear and cheerful, yes, cheerful in spite of everything and anything.' It would be quite uplifting if we would once more embrace this as a guiding principle.

'Enthusiasm combined with critical thought—what more could we want of ourselves!' Rosa Luxemburg wrote optimistically in one of her last letters to Adolf Warksy in December 1918. It wasn't enough. This fine phrase, which adorned the house where she was born in Zamość, was removed a few years ago by Polish authorities in a frantic attempt to quell renewed interest in her life and work. It's important not to let this happen and to utilize the new interest in her work to examine the 'lost treasure' of her revolution, as Arendt once described popular councils, and explore its possibilities. Why don't we start experimenting with a new form of citizen councils to inject more democracy into society?

It might just avoid a return to 'dark times.' Rosa Luxemburg and Hannah Arendt give us hope because they can clarify, assess, and illuminate the times we live in. They help us to understand the events that occurred before we entered the world, enabling us to 'learn' from history and be better prepared for new beginnings in the future. 'Understanding is specifically the human way of being alive,' Arendt wrote. Both Arendt and Luxemburg are important voices from the past, history's not yet 'lost treasures.' They were far ahead of their time because they thought and wrote in the vanguard, from the *nunc stans*—the eternal moment—breaching the divide between an elapsed past and a future yet to unfold. They both offer enduring inspiration because the original and human power of their thinking touches and so animates us.

A Selection of
Rosa Luxemburg's Letters
from Prison between
December 1916 and
December 1917

To Mathilde Wurm

Wronke, December 28, 1916

My dearest Tilde!

I want to answer your Christmas letter immediately, while the anger it stirred up in me is still fresh. Yes, your letter made me hopping mad, because every line in it, brief as it is, shows how very much you are again under the spell of your milieu.[1] This crybaby tone, this 'oh dear' and 'woe is me' about the 'disappointments' you've experienced—attributing them to others, instead of just looking at the mirror to see all the wretchedness of humanity in its most striking likeness! And in your mouth 'we' now means the froggy denizens of the swamp [i.e., the centrists] with whom you now associate, whereas earlier, when you were with me, 'we' meant in company with me. So just wait, and I'll deal with you [*Dich*—singular, familiar] in plural terms [*per 'Ihr'*—in the plural of 'you'; 'you-all'; 'all of you'].

You suppose, in your melancholy way, that you are 'too little of an adventure-goer' for my taste. 'Too little' is good! Generally speaking, all of you are not 'goers' but 'creepers.' It is not a difference of degree, but of substance. In general, 'you-all' [*'Ihr'*] are of a different zoological genus from me, and you-all's peevish, sour-puss, cowardly, and half-hearted way of being was never so foreign and so hateful to me as now. You suggest that 'adventure-going' would indeed be suitable for you-all, but one merely gets put 'in the hole' for

Except where noted, the letters that follow are taken from *The Letters of Rosa Luxemburg* by Rosa Luxemburg, first published by Verso 2011, © Verso 2011, 2013.

1. Luxemburg is referring to the milieu of the centrist opposition in German Social Democracy, grouped around Karl Kautsky.

that, and is then 'of little use.' Oh, you miserable pettifogging souls, who would certainly be ready for a bit of 'heroism,' but only for cash, for at least three moldy copper pennies, because you first have to see 'something of use' lying on the store counter. And for you people the simple statement of honorable and straightforward men, 'Here I stand, I can do no other, so help me God,' was never spoken. It's lucky that world history up to now was not made by people like all of you, because otherwise we would have had no Reformation and would probably still be sitting under the *ancien régime*. As for me, in recent times I, who certainly was never soft, have become as hard as polished steel and from now on will neither politically nor in personal relations make even the slightest concession. When I simply recall the gallery of your heroes, such a fit of depression takes hold of me [to think of them]: the sweet-spoken Haase, Dittmann with his lovely beard and lovely Reichstag speeches, and the wavering, misguided shepherd Kautsky, who your Emmo[2] follows loyally, of course, over hill and dale, the magnificent Arthur [Stadthagen]—*ah, je n'en finirai!*[3] I swear to you: I would rather sit for years [in prison]—and I don't mean here [in Wronke], where after all it's like being in the kingdom of heaven, but rather in the cave at Alexanderplatz where I, in an eleven square meter cell, without light both mornings and evenings, crammed in between the C (without W) and the iron bunk, would recite my Mörike aloud—I would rather do that than 'fight,' if I can use the term, beside your heroes, or in general have anything to do with them! Indeed I would rather deal with Count Westarp—and not because

2. The nickname of Emmanuel Wurm, Mathilde Wurm's husband.
3. French: 'oh, I could never finish [the list].'

he spoke of my 'almond-shaped velvet eyes' in the Reichstag, but because he is a man. I tell you, as soon as I can stick my nose out of here again, I will come hunting and hounding your company of frogs with the blare of trumpets, the cracking of whips, and the baying of bloodhounds—I was going to say, like Penthesilea,[4] but by God the bunch of you are by no means Achilles. Have you had enough of my New Year's greeting yet? Then see that you remain a human being. To be a human being is the main thing, above all else. And that means: to be firm and clear and cheerful, yes, cheerful in spite of everything and anything, because howling is the business of the weak. To be a human being means to joyfully toss your entire life 'on the giant scales of fate' if it must be so, and at the same time to rejoice in the brightness of every day and the beauty of every cloud. Oh, I don't know any recipe that can be written down on how to be a human being, I only know when a person is one, and you too always used to know when we walked together through the fields of Südende for hours at a time and the red glow of evening lay upon the stalks of grain. The world is so beautiful, with all its horrors, and would be even more beautiful if there were no weaklings or cowards in it. Come, you get another kiss, after all, because you actually are an honorable, well-intentioned little girl. A toast to the new year! R.

---

4. In ancient Greek myth, queen of the Amazons, who fought against and is killed by Achilles in the Trojan War. In Heinrich von Kleist's play *Penthesilea*, which Luxemburg directly refers to in another letter, Penthesilea kills Achilles.

To Luise Kautsky

Wronke in Poznań, Fortress, January 26, 1917

Lulu, beloved! Yesterday in Berlin I had a hearing (in my absence), at which undoubtedly a few months of prison have again fallen to my lot.[1] Today it has been exactly three months that I have been stuck 'sitting' here—in the third stage [of my imprisonment].[2] In celebration of two such memorable days, by which they have interrupted my existence in this pleasant way for years now, you deserve to get a letter. Forgive me, dearest, for letting you wait so long for an answer from me, but I just had a bout of miserable cowardice for a short time. For several days we had an icy wind storm, and I felt so tiny and weak that I didn't go out of my 'den' at all, for fear that the cold would totally destroy me. In such a mood I was of course waiting for a warm-hearted, encouraging letter, but unfortunately my friends always wait to be prodded and nudged by me. None of them ever take a good fresh initiative and write me of their own accord— other than Hänschen [Diefenbach]. He [Hans Diefenbach] is probably rather tired by now after two and a half years

1. Charges were brought against Luxemburg before the Royal Special Court in central Berlin for insulting an officer of the criminal justice system. She was sentenced to an additional ten days in prison.

2. The first 'stage' was in the prison at Alexanderplatz, the second was at the women's prison on Barnim Street, and the third was at Wronke. On July 10, 1916, because of her political activity, Luxemburg was taken into 'military protective custody' by order of General Gustav von Kessel, the top military commander of the March of Brandenburg. At first she was held in the police prison at Alexanderplatz in Berlin, then on July 21, she was moved to the Berlin women's prison on Barnim Street. From October 26, 1916, to July 22, 1917, she was held in the Wronke fortress in the province of Poznań. From there she was sent to the Breslau prison, from which she was finally freed by the German revolution on November 8, 1918.

of writing letters 'that don't reach you' and that are not answered. Finally a letter came from Sonya [Liebknecht], but her tone is always like that of cracked glass. At that point I hastened, as always, to get back up out of the depths by my own effort, and it is good to do that.

Now I am bright and lively again and in a good mood, and the only way you're failing me is that you're not here chitchatting and laughing as only the two of us understand how to do. I would very soon get you laughing again, even though your last few letters sounded disturbingly gloomy. You know, once when we were coming home from an evening at Bebel's and around midnight in the middle of the street three of us were putting on a regular frog's concert, you said that when we two were together you always felt a little tipsy, as though we had been drinking bubbly. That's exactly what I love about you, that I can always put you in a champagne mood, with life making our fingers tingle and us ready for any kind of foolishness. We can go without seeing each other for three years, and then within half an hour it's as though we'd seen each other only yesterday, and I would so much like right now to suddenly break in on Hans Naivus [Hans Kautsky] and be able to laugh again with you and those sitting around your table, the way we laughed in June during the visit by Hänschen [Diefenbach]. (He wrote me later that in the train all the way to the front he had to laugh out loud from time to time to the amazement of his soldier comrades in the railroad compartment and undoubtedly 'looked like an idiot' in their eyes.) Actual champagne is out of the question and has been now for a long time, ever since poor [Hugo] Faisst fell as the first casualty of the World War.[3]

3. Hugo Faisst died on July 30, 1914.

Well, away with champagne and away with the *Lieder* of Hugo Wolf. By the way I have a very heart-warming memory of our last 'carousal' with champagne. It was in the last summer [before the war] when I was in the Black Forest.[4] He [Faisst] came on a Sunday with Costia [i.e., Kostya Zetkin], they having clambered up from Wildbad for a visit; it was a marvelous day and after eating, we sat out in the open around a small battery of bottles of Mumm [champagne], we rejoiced in the sun and were very merry. Of course the one who drank the most was 'the noble donor' [of the champagne, i.e., Faisst]. Once again he experienced 'an unforgettable hour,' laughing, gesticulating, crying out, and shoving one sparkling glass after the other into his wide-open Swabian 'trap.' He was especially amused by the Sunday visiting public that swarmed around us on the porch. 'Look how these Philistines are gaping at us,' he cried out enthusiastically, 'if only they knew who was going on a bender here!' And the funniest thing was that we were the ones who were clueless, because the landlord, as he told me later that evening, had somehow deciphered my unfortunate 'incognito' and naturally tipped off all his guests about it. The scoundrel kept serving us with such ingratiating smiles and made the corks pop extra loud, but the Philistines were, as you can imagine, most highly edified by this 'Social Democratic champagne orgy.'—And now for the third time already over Faisst's grave the springtime will 'let its blue ribbon flutter' (he sang that song[5] very beautifully, much better than Ju-

---

4. Rosa Luxemburg is probably referring to the time she spent at Wiesenbach in the Black Forest. She was there together with Clara Zetkin in August 1912.

5. The reference is to Eduard Mörike's poem 'Er ist's' (He's the One), set to music by the composer Hugo Wolf.

lia Culp, whom we once heard—do you still remember?—
once when you and I were together at the Academy of Song).
Probably for you the desire for music, as for all other things,
has gone by for a while, your mind is full of concern about
world history, which has gone all wrong, and your heart is
full of sighs over the wretchedness of—Scheidemann and
comrades. And everyone who writes to me moans and sighs
in the same way. Don't you understand that the overall disaster is much too great to be moaned and groaned about? I
can grieve or feel bad if Mimi is sick, or if you are not well.
But when the whole world is out of joint, then I merely seek
to understand what is going on and why, and then I have
done my duty, and I am calm and in good spirits from then
on. *Ultra posse nemo obligatur.*[6] And then for me there still
remains everything else that makes me happy: music and
painting and clouds and doing botany in the spring and good
books and Mimi and you and much more.—In short, I am
'stinking rich' and I'm thinking of staying that way to the
end. This giving oneself up completely to the headaches and
miseries of the day is completely incomprehensible and intolerable to me. See, for example, how Goethe stood above
things with cool composure. But think what he must have
gone through: the Great French Revolution, which surely
must have seemed like a bloody and completely pointless
farce from up close, and then from 1793 till 1815 an unbro-
ken series of wars, when once again the world must have
seemed like a madhouse turned loose. Yet at the same time
how calmly, with such equanimity, he pursued his studies
about the metamorphosis of plants, the theory of colors, and
a thousand other things. I don't ask that you be a poet like

6. Latin: 'None are obliged to do more than they can.'

Goethe, but everyone can adopt for themselves his outlook on life—the universalism of interests, the inner harmony—or at least strive toward that. And if you say something like: but Goethe was not a political fighter, my opinion is this: a fighter is precisely a person who must strive to rise above things, otherwise one's nose will get stuck in every bit of nonsense.—Obviously I'm thinking of a fighter on the grand scale, not a weathervane of the caliber of the 'great men' who sit around your table, who recently sent a greeting card to me here. . . . Never mind[7]—your greeting was really the only one that was dear to me among all those. And in recompense for that I want to send you very soon a little picture from my Turner album. The only thing is that you better not give me a rebuff in reply to that, as recently occurred for me. Just think, for Christmas I sent a wonderfully beautiful picture from this album to Leo [Jogiches] and then I received word by way of Miss Jacob: refused with thanks; supposedly it was 'vandalism,' and the picture must be replaced in the album! Typical Leo, isn't that so? I was furious, because I also hold the view that Goethe expresses here:

> Would I have any hesitation,
> From Balkh, Bukhara, Samarkand,
> These cities' brightest, shiny goods
> To send to you, my love so grand?
> Or would you rather ask the king
> To grant you these cities from above?
> He's more magnificent and wiser,
> But he knows not how to love.[8]

7. These two words were written in English.
8. These lines are from Goethe's *West-East Divan*.

Leo [Jogiches] is neither the king nor 'wiser,' but still 'he knows not how to love.' And yet the two of us know, don't we, Lulu? And when I next have the chance to pull down a few stars to bestow on someone for use as cufflinks, there better be no cold-blooded pedant with his finger raised to restrain me, saying that I'm creating confusion in all the astronomy textbooks.

. . . I am definitely ordering up a visit from you for the spring. You will be astounded by everything you will find here around me. The great titmice are in loyal attendance in front of my window, they already know my voice exactly, and it seems that they like it when I sing. Recently I sang the Countess's aria from *Figaro*, about six of them were perched there on a bush in front of the window and listened without moving all the way to the end; it was a very funny sight to see. Then there are also two blackbirds that come at my call every day, I've never seen such tame ones. They eat out of the metal plate in front of the window. For this purpose I have ordered a cantata also to be held on April 1 [April Fool's Day], which should be quite an event. Can't you send me some sunflower seeds for these little people? And for my own beak I would also like to order another 'military cake,' like the ones you've already sent a few times, they provide one with a slight foretaste of paradise. And now that I'm talking about lofty and super-lofty things, there's one more problem that gives me no rest: it seems that the world of the stars has gone all wrong, without my being to blame. I don't know for sure if you have noticed in the midst of your intense concern about Scheidemann, but last year an epoch-making discovery was revealed: the Englishman Walkey is said to have discovered 'the center of the universe,' and supposedly it's the star Canopus in the constellation Argo (in the southern hemisphere), which is 'only' five hundred light years away from us and is approximately 1.5 million times larger than the sun. These dimensions don't impress me at all, I have become blasé. But I'm concerned about something else: a single center around which 'everything' moves transforms the universe into a kind of round ball. Now I find it completely far-fetched to imagine the universe as a ball—a kind of giant potato dumpling or *bombe glacé*. The symmetry of such an image, when applied 'to the whole,' seems to me a completely fatuous petty-bourgeois conception. Since we are talking about nothing more and nothing less than the infinity of the universe, this is like thumbing one's nose at the concept [of infinity]. Because a 'ball-shaped infinity' is certainly rubbish. And for my own spiritual comfort I must think of the infinite as something other than human stupidity! As you see, I literally have the 'worries and concerns of the philosopher Kant.' What does Hans Naivus think about this or his learned son [*filius*]? Now write a proper letter right away *de omnibus rebus*,[9] otherwise I will evict you from the main chamber of my heart, where you now sit right next to Mimi, and put you in a side chamber.—

Good Lord! I forgot the main thing: I have not yet finished the translation.[10] Only seven signatures [*Bogen*] remain to be finished, but first I must make a clean copy [of

9. Latin: 'about all things.'

10. Luxemburg was translating from Russian to German the autobiographical novel by Vladimir Korolenko, *Istoriia moego sovremen-nika* (History of My Contemporary). Her translation was brought out posthumously in Berlin in 1919 by Paul Cassirer Publishers. She wrote her introduction to this book in July 1918 while in prison in Breslau; the German text of the introduction is in her *Gesammelte Werke*, vol. 4, pp. 302–31.

the drafts]. Can't the publisher make a judgment based on the twelve 'signatures'?! But finally I must close.

I embrace you, your R.

N.B.: You can write directly to this address: Wronke i. P. [in Poznań], the Fortress, I will certainly get the letter.

If you receive a letter for me from Hänschen [Diefenbach], send it here without worrying. He can write to me about everything.

To Marta Rosenbaum

[Wronke, between February 4 and 9, 1917]
My dear Martchen![1]

I was so happy about your visit yesterday. It was so lovely, so comfortable and friendly, and I certainly hope that today and Sunday will be the same. For me your visit gives great refreshment to my soul, and I will now draw nourishment from it for many weeks to come. You provide so much healing warmth with your nearness, you dear soul. After a little while you'll come again, won't you? I'm already rejoicing over the next time. That is, if I continue to sit [in confinement] here. But in general you can feel at peace about me, really: I am now following the doctor's orders with the most painful exactness and have the firm hope of leaving here healthy and strong, so that you will find it a joy to see me at work and in battle. There will be very, very much work and battling to do. But I absolutely do not become disheartened. Dearest, history itself always knows best what to do about things, even when the situation looks most desperate. I speak this word not as some sort of comfortable fatalism! Quite the opposite! The human will must be spurred on to the utmost, and it's necessary to fight consciously with all one's might. What I mean is: The success of such conscious effort toward influencing the masses now, when everything seems so totally hopeless, depends on the deep, elemental, hidden wellsprings of history, and I know from the lessons of history as well as from my personal experience in Russia that it is precisely when everything has the outward appearance of being terrible with absolutely no way out, just then

1. Diminutive, endearing form of Marta.

a complete turnaround is being prepared, is in the making, and it proves to be all the more powerful because of [the delay]. In general, don't ever forget: We are linked with the laws of historical development, and these never fail, even if sometimes they don't go exactly according to some 'plan F' that we have worked out. And so, in all eventualities: Hold your head high and don't let your courage fail.

I embrace you heartily with warmth and love, Your R.

[P.S.] Please also write to Hänschen [Diefenbach], [to say that] in the event that, as I suggest, he simply wants to show up here, then Sunday afternoon is best. Perhaps next Sunday? Of course he should not mention that he knew Sunday would be best, he should just come 'on the off chance,' because permission from the commandant takes too long. I guarantee that it will work.

To Mathilde Wurm

Wronke i. P., Fortress
February 16, 1917

(Send your letters directly here sealed and without the notation 'prisoner-of-war letter.')

My dear Tilde!

Letter, postcard, and cookies received—many thanks. Be at peace; despite the fact that you so boldly parried my thrust and are even challenging me to a duel,[1] I remain as kindly disposed toward you as ever. I had to laugh that you want to 'engage in combat' with me. Girl, I sit firmly in the saddle, no one yet has stretched me out on the sand; I would be interested to see the one who can do it. It was for a different reason, though, that I had to smile: because you really don't want to 'engage in combat' with me at all, and you even depend on me politically more than you want to believe is true. I will always remain a compass for you, because your very nature tells you that I have the most unerring judgment— in my case all the distracting side issues fall away: anxiety or nervousness, routinism, parliamentary cretinism, things that color the judgment of others. You argue against my slogan, 'Here I stand—I can do no other!' Your argument comes down to the following: that is all well and good, but human beings are too cowardly and weak for such heroism, ergo one must adapt one's tactics to their weakness and to the principle *che va piano, va sano*.[2] What narrowness of historical outlook, my little lamb! There is nothing more change-

---

1. See above, the letter to Mathilde Wurm of December 28, 1916.
2. The Italian phrase means literally 'whoever walks softly, walks sensibly'; an equivalent English phrase is 'slow but sure.'

able than human psychology. That's especially because the psyche of the masses, like Thalatta,[3] the eternal sea, always bears within it every latent possibility: deathly stillness and raging storm, the basest cowardice and the wildest heroism. The masses are always what they must be according to the circumstances of the times, and they are always on the verge of becoming something totally different from what they seem to be. It would be a fine sea captain who would steer a course based only on the momentary appearance of the ocean's surface and did not understand how to draw conclusions from signs in the sky and in the ocean's depths. My dear little girl, 'disappointment with the masses' is always the most reprehensible quality to be found in a political leader. A leader with the quality of greatness applies tactics, not according to the momentary mood of the masses, but according to higher laws of development, and sticks firmly to those tactics despite all disappointments and, for the rest, calmly allows history to bring its work to fruition.

With that let us close the debate. I willingly remain your friend.

Whether I also remain a teacher for you, as you want, depends on you.

You reminisce about an evening six years ago when we were waiting by the shore of the Schlachtensee [a lake in Berlin] for the comet to appear.[4] Oddly enough, I have absolutely no recollection of that. But you have awakened another memory for me. At that time on an October evening I was sitting with Hans Kautsky (the painter) by the Havel River, across from the Peacock Island, and we were also

3. The Greek word for sea is *thalassa*.
4. The reference was to Halley's comet, which was visible in 1910.

waiting to see the comet. The twilight had already deep-
ened, but on the horizon a dim reddish-purple strip was still
aglow, and it was mirrored in the Havel, transforming the
surface of the water into a vast enormous rose petal. Across
the way a buoy sounded softly, and in one area the water was
sprinkled with many dark spots. These were wild ducks, who
were taking a rest from their flight along the Havel, and their
muffled cry, in which there is so much longing and a sense
of vast, empty expanse—they were conveying that cry across
the water to us. The mood was wonderful, and we were sitting there in silence as though entranced. I was looking toward the Havel River. Hans happened to be looking at me
[with his back to the river]. Suddenly he behaved as though
he were appalled and grasped me by the hand: What was
wrong with me? he cried out. Behind his back a meteor had
fallen and had flooded me with a green phosphorous light so
that I looked as pale green as a corpse, and because I started
and had a strikingly startled expression on my face, because
of the same spectacle [behind his back] that he could not
see, Hans probably thought I was having a fatal attack and
was dying. (Later he created a beautiful big painting of that
evening on the Havel.)

To me it is disastrous that you now have no time or mood
for anything but 'item number one,' namely the miserable
state of the party, because such one-sidedness also clouds
one's political judgment, and above all one must at all times
live as a complete human being. But look here, girl, if the
fact is that you seldom get around to picking up a book, then
at least read only the good ones, not such kitsch as the 'Spi-
noza novel' which you sent me. What do you want with this
theme of the 'special suffering of the Jews'? I am just as much
concerned with the poor victims on the rubber plantations
of Putumayo, the Blacks in Africa with whose corpses the

Europeans play catch. You know the words that were written about the great work of the General Staff, about Gen. Trotha's campaign in the Kalahari desert:[5] 'And the death rattles of the dying, the demented cries of those driven mad by thirst faded away in the sublime stillness of eternity.' Oh that 'sublime stillness of eternity,' in which so many cries of anguish have faded away unheard, they resound within me so strongly that I have no special place in my heart for the [Jewish] ghetto. I feel at home in the entire world, wherever there are clouds and birds and human tears.

Yesterday evening there were amazingly beautiful pink clouds above the walls of my fortress. I stood in front of my grated window and recited to myself my favorite poem by Mörike:

Into a friendly city I came one day.

Along its streets the ruddy glow of sunset lay.

From an open window just then,

Across a most luxuriant spread of flowers,

Far off I heard the golden trembling of bells,

And a single human voice had the sound of a nightingale
    chorus,

So that all the flowers quivered,

5. In 1904, in German Southwest Africa, the Herero and Hottentot peoples rose up against the harsh colonial rule of German imperialism. To put down the uprising a force of 12,000 colonial troops was deployed under the command of General Lothar von Trotha. The indigenous people were driven out into the desert, cut off from their sources of water, and as a result tens of thousands were left to die a horrible death. General von Trotha also gave orders to shoot and kill women and children. Earlier, in 1900, Von Trotha had commanded a German brigade during the suppression of the Boxer Rebellion in China; an alliance of Western governments employed mass murder to put it down. Von Trotha later became a leading member of the racist Tule Society, which greatly influenced the young Adolf Hitler.

So that all fragrances became more vivid,
So that a higher redness touched the rose.
Long was I held there, dazed with delight, astonished.
How I came out of the city gates,
To tell the truth, I do not know myself.
And here—how lightly lies the world around me.
The heavens heave with crowds decked out in purple,
The city's in a golden haze, behind me.
How the stream roars amidst its alder bushes!
How the ground groans with the grinding millstones!
Like one who's drunk too much, I'm at a loss.
O Muse, you've moved my heart to tears,
With your silken fetters of love!

And so, may life treat you well, my fine young girl. Heaven knows when I'll have a chance to write you again. Nowadays I have no inclination for writing. But I owed you this one.

I send you a kiss and a hearty squeeze of the hand, your R.

To Sophie Liebknecht

Wronke, February 18, 1917

My dearest Sonyichka,

... It is long since I have been shaken by anything as by Martha's brief report of your visit to Karl, how you had to see him through a grating, and the impression it made on you. Why didn't you tell me about it? I have a right to share in anything which hurts you, and I wouldn't allow anyone to curtail my proprietary rights!

Besides, Martha's account reminded me so vividly of the first time my brother and my sister came to see me ten years ago in the Warsaw citadel. There they put you in a regular cage consisting of two layers of wire mesh; or rather, a small cage stands freely inside a larger one, and the prisoner only sees the visitor through this double trellis-work. It was just at the end of a six-day hunger strike, and I was so weak that the commanding officer of the fortress had almost to carry me into the visitors' room. I had to hold on with both hands to the wires of the cage, and this must certainly have strengthened the resemblance to a wild beast in the zoo. The cage was standing in a rather dark corner of the room, and my brother pressed his face against the wires. 'Where are you?,' he kept on asking, continually wiping away the tears that clouded his glasses.—How glad I should be if I could only take Karl's place in the cage of Luckau prison, so as to save him from such an ordeal!

Convey my most grateful thanks to Pfemfert for Galswor-

The translation of this letter is taken from the Luxemburg Internet Archive 2005, available at https://www.marxists.org/archive/luxemburg/1918/letters-sophie.htm.

thy's book. I finished it yesterday, and liked it so much. Not as much as *The Man of Property*. It pleased me less, precisely because in it social criticism is more preponderant. When I am reading a novel I am less concerned with any moral it may convey than with its purely artistic merits. What troubles me in the case of *Fraternity* is that Galsworthy's intelligence overburdens the book. This criticism will surprise you. I regard Galsworthy as of the same type as Bernard Shaw and Oscar Wilde, a type which now has many representatives among the British intelligentsia. They are able, ultracivilized, a trifle bored with the world, and they are inclined to regard everything with a humorous skepticism. The subtly ironical remarks that Galsworthy makes concerning his own dramatis personae, while remaining himself apparently quite serious, often make me burst out laughing. But persons who are truly well-bred rarely or never make fun of their own associates, even though they do not fail to note anything ludicrous; in like manner, a supreme artist never makes a butt of his own creations.

Don't misunderstand me, Sonichka; don't think that I am objecting to satire in the grand style! For example, Gerhart Hauptmann's[1] *Emanuel Quint* is the most ferocious satire of modern society that has been written for a hundred years. But the author himself is not on the grin as he writes. At the close he stands with lips atremble, and the tears glisten in his widely open eyes. Galsworthy, on the other hand, with his smartly phrased interpolations, makes me feel as I have felt at an evening party when my neighbor, as each new

1. German dramatist, born 1862. The best known of his numerous plays, *The Weavers*, published in 1892, had as its theme the Silesian labor troubles of the year 1844.

guest has entered, has whispered some appropriate piece of spite into my ear . . .

This is Sunday, the deadliest of days for prisoners and solitaries. I am sad at heart, but I earnestly hope that both you and Karl are free from care. Write soon to let me know when and where you are at length going for a change.

All my love to you and the children.

Your Rosa

Do you think Pfemfert could send me something else worth reading? Perhaps one of Thomas Mann's' books?[2] I have not read any of them yet.

One more request. I am beginning to find the sun rather trying when I go out; could you send me a yard of black spotted veiling? Thanks in advance.

2. German novelist, born 1875. His favorite topic is the life of the rich mercantile class of Hamburg.

To Sophie Liebknecht

Breslau, August 2, 1917

My dearest Sonyichka,

Your letter, which I received on the 28th [of July], was the first news that reached me here from the outside world, and you can easily imagine how very happy it made me. In your affectionate anxiety about me you definitely take too tragic a view of my relocation.[1] After all, the likes of us are constantly living 'one step at a time,' and as you know, I take all the twists and turns of fate with the necessary cheerful equanimity. I have already settled in here quite well, my boxes of books arrived from Wronke today, and so my two cells here will soon be looking just as homelike and comfortable as were my quarters there, with my books and pictures unpacked, along with the modest ornaments that I like to carry around with me, and soon I will get down to work with redoubled pleasure. Of course what I don't have here is the relative freedom of movement I had at Wronke, where during the day the fortress was wide open, whereas here I am simply locked up, and then I'm also lacking the glorious fresh air, the garden, and, above all, the birds! You have no idea how much I came to depend on the society of those little creatures. However, one can of course do without all that, and soon I will forget that I ever had it any better. The whole situation here is almost exactly like it was at Barnim Street, except that there I had the lovely green infirmary garden in which every day I could make some new little discov-

1. On July 22, 1917, Luxemburg had been transferred from the Wronke fortress to a prison in Breslau (then the capital of Silesia, on the Oder River).

ery in botany or zoology. There is no chance of 'discovering' anything here in the great paved courtyard, which only
serves for taking walks, and as I go back and forth, I keep
my eyes riveted on the gray paving stones to spare myself
the sight of the prisoners at work in the yard, who, in their
demeaning prison clothes, it is always a pain for me to look
at, and among whom a few are always to be found whose
age, gender, or individual features have been blotted out under the stamp of the most profound human degradation, but
who, by the force of some sort of painful magnetism, always
catch my eye. Everywhere, of course, there are also individual figures from whom even the prison clothes do not de-
tract and who would gladden the eye of any painter. Thus
I have already discovered a young working woman here in
the prison yard whose slender form and concise gestures,
with her head wrapped in a kerchief and the austerity of her
profile, is a direct embodiment of a figure painted by Millet;
it is a pleasure to see the nobility of movement with which
she carries her loads, and her gaunt face with the unvary-
ing chalk-white complexion reminds one of a tragic Pierrot
mask. However, made wiser by sad experience, I try to give
a wide berth to such highly promising manifestations. The
thing is that at Barnim Street I came across a woman prisoner of truly queenly appearance and bearing, and I thought
to myself that there must be a corresponding 'interior.' Then
she came to my part of the prison as an odd-job worker
[*Kalfaktrice*], and after two days it became evident that beneath the beautiful mask there lay such a mass of stupidity,
such a base mentality, that from then on I always averted
my gaze when she crossed my path. It occurred to me then
that, ultimately, Venus de Milo could only have earned her
reputation over thousands of years as the most beautiful of

women only because she was silent. Had she opened her mouth, it might perhaps have come to light that at bottom she was like some women of limited mentality who take in washing or sewing, and the entire charm of her person would have gone to the devil.

What I see from my window is the men's prison, the usual gloomy building of red brick. But looking diagonally, I can see above the prison wall the green treetops of some kind of park. One of them is a tall black poplar, which I can hear rustling when the wind blows hard; and there is a row of ash trees, much lighter in color, and covered with yellow clusters of seedpods (later they will be dark brown). The windows look to the northwest, so that I often see splendid sunsets, and you know how the sight of rose-tinted clouds can carry me away from everything and make up for all else. At 8 p.m. (according to [the special] 'summer time,' in reality, 7 p.m.)[2] the sun has only just sunk behind the gables of the men's prison; it still shines right through the skylights on the roof, and the entire heavens have a golden glow. I feel so happy then, and something—I know not what—makes me sing softly to myself the 'Ave Maria' by Gounod (you know it of course).

Many thanks for copying out the items by Goethe. [The poem] 'Men of Entitlement' [*Die berechtigten Männer*] is really very fine, although I had never been struck by it before; we are all open to suggestion in our judgment of something's beauty. If you have time, I wish you would copy out for me 'Anacreon's Grave' [*Anakreons Grab*] by Goethe. Do you know it well? Hugo Wolf composed a song [*Lied*] from it, which

2. In Germany in 1917, from April 16 to September 17, there was a special summer reckoning of time by which all clocks were set one hour ahead of the standard time (equivalent to daylight savings time in the USA).

first enabled me to really understand it. Set to music, it conveys an architectonic quality: One seems to see a Greek temple rise before one's eyes.

You ask, 'How does one become good?' How does one get the 'subaltern demon' inside oneself to be quiet? Sonyichka, I don't know any way other than to link up with the cheerfulness and beauty of life which are always around us everywhere, if one only knows how to use one's eyes and ears, and thus to create an inner equilibrium and rise above everything petty and annoying.

Just now the sun—I took a little break from writing, to observe the heavens—has dropped much lower behind the [men's prison] building, and high up in the sky, myriads of little clouds have silently assembled—God knows from where—their edges have a silvery sheen, but in the middle they are a soft gray, and with all their ragged outlines they are heading north. In this procession of clouds there is so much smiling unconcern that I have to smile along with them, just as I always go along with the rhythm of life around me. With the presence of a sky like this, how could one possibly be 'bad' or petty? As long as you never forget to look around you, you will always be 'good' without fail.

It surprises me a little that Karl [Liebknecht] wants a book specifically about bird calls. For me the voice of the birds is inseparable from their habitat and their life as a whole, it is only the whole that interests me, rather than any detached detail. Give him a good book on the geographical distribution of animals, which will certainly give him a lot of stimulation.

I hope you will soon come to visit me. Send me a telegram as soon as you have permission to visit.

I embrace you many times, your R.

To Sophie Liebknecht

Breslau, mid-November 1917
My beloved Sonichka,

I hope soon to have a chance of sending you this letter at long last, so I hasten to take up my pen. For how long a time I have been forced to forbear my habit of talking to you—on paper at least. I am allowed to write so few letters, and I had to save up my chances for Hans D. [Diefenbach] who was expecting to hear from me. But now all is over. My last two letters to him were addressed to a dead man, and one has already been returned to me. His loss still seems incredible. But enough of this. I prefer to consider such matters in solitude. It only annoys me beyond expression when people try, as N. tried, 'to break the news' to me, and to make a parade of their own grief by way of 'consolation.' Why should my closest friends understand me so little and hold me so cheaply as to be unable to realize that the best way in such cases is to say quickly, briefly, and simply: 'He is dead'?

... How I deplore the loss of all these months and years in which we might have had so many joyful hours together, notwithstanding all the horrors that are going on throughout the world. Do you know, Sonichka, the longer it lasts, and the more the infamy and monstrosity of the daily happenings surpasses all bounds, the more tranquil and more confident becomes my personal outlook. I say to myself that it is absurd to apply moral standards to the great elemental forces that manifest themselves in a hurricane, a flood, or

The translation of this letter is taken from the Luxemburg Internet Archive 2005, available at https://www.marxists.org/archive/luxemburg/1917/undated/02.htm.

an eclipse of the sun. We have to accept them simply as data for investigation, as subjects of study.

. . . Manifestly, objectively considered, these are the only possible lines along which history can move, and we must follow the movement without losing sight of the main trend. I have the feeling that all this moral filth through which we are wading, this huge madhouse in which we live, may all of a sudden, between one day and the next, be transformed into its very opposite, as if by the stroke of a magician's wand may become something stupendously great and heroic; must inevitable be so transformed, if only the war lasts a few years longer.

. . . Read Anatole France's *The Gods Are Athirst*. My main reason for admiring this work so much is because the author, with the insight of genius into all that is universally human, seems to say to us: 'Behold, out of these petty personalities, out of these trivial commonplaces, arise, when the hour is ripe, the most titanic events and the most monumental gestures of history.' We have to take everything as it comes both in social life and in private life; to accept what happens, tranquilly, comprehensively, and with a smile. I feel absolutely convinced that things will take the right turn when the war ends, or not long afterwards; but obviously we have first to pass through a period of terrible human suffering.

What I have just written reminds me of an incident I wish to tell you of, for it seems to me so poetical and so touching. I was recently reading a scientific work upon the migrations of birds, a phenomenon which has hitherto seemed rather enigmatic. From this I learned that certain species, which at ordinary times live at enmity one with another (because some are birds of prey, whilst others are victims), will keep the peace during their great southward flight across the sea. Among the birds that come to winter in Egypt—come in such numbers that the sky is darkened by their flight—are, besides hawks, eagles, falcons, and owls, thousands of little song birds such as larks, golden-crested wrens, and nightingales, mingling fearlessly with the great birds of prey. A 'truce of God' seems to have been declared for the journey. All are striving toward the common goal, to drop, half dead from fatigue, in the land of the Nile and subsequently to assort themselves by species and localities. Nay more, during the long flight the larger birds have been seen to carry smaller birds on their backs, for instance, cranes have passed in great numbers with a twittering freight of small birds of passage. Is not that charming?

. . . In a tasteless jumble of poems I was looking at recently, I came across one by Hugo von Hoffmannsthal. As a rule I do not care for his writings, I consider them artificial, stilted, and obscure; I simply can't understand him, But this poem is an exception; it pleased me greatly and made a strong impression on me. I am sending you a copy of it, for I think you will like it too.

I am now deep in the study of geology. Perhaps you will think that must be a dry subject, but if so, you are mistaken. I am reading it with intense interest and passionate enjoyment; it opens up such wide intellectual vistas and supplies a more perfectly united and more comprehensive conception of nature than any other science. There are so many things I should like to tell you about it, but for that we should have to have a real talk, taking a morning stroll together through the country at the South End, or seeing one another home several times in succession on a calm moonlit night. What are you reading now? How are you getting on with the *The*

Lessing Legend?[1] I want to know everything about you. Write at once, if you can, by the same route; or, failing that, by the official route, without mentioning this letter. I am already counting the weeks till I can hope to see you here again. I suppose it will be soon after the New Year?

What news have you from Karl? When do you expect to see him? Give him a thousand greetings from me. All my love to you, my dear, dear Sonichka. Write soon and copiously.

Your Rosa

1. A book by Franz Mehring

To Sophie Liebknecht

Breslau, before December 24, 1917

... This is my third Christmas in the clink, but you should certainly not take that tragically. I am as calm and cheerful as ever. . . . I'm lying here in a dark cell on a stone-hard mattress, the usual silence of a church cemetery prevails in the prison building, it seems as though we're in a tomb; on the ceiling can be seen reflections coming through the window from the lanterns that burn all night in front of the prison. From time to time one hears, but only in quite a muffled way, the distant rumbling of a train passing by or quite nearby under the windows the whispering of the guards on duty at night, who take a few steps slowly in their heavy boots to relieve their stiff legs. The sand crunches so hopelessly under their heels that the entire hopeless wasteland of existence can be heard in this damp, dark night. I lie there quietly, alone, wrapped in these many-layered black veils of darkness, boredom, lack of freedom, and winter—and at the same time my heart is racing with an incomprehensible, unfamiliar inner joy as though I were walking across a flowering meadow in radiant sunshine. And in the dark I smile at life, as if I knew some sort of magical secret that gives the lie to everything evil and sad and changes it into pure light and happiness. . . . I believe that the secret is nothing other than life itself; the deep darkness of night is so beautiful and as soft as velvet, if one only looks at it the right way; and in the crunching of the damp sand beneath the slow, heavy steps of the sentries a beautiful small song of life is being sung—if one only knows how to listen properly. At such moments I think of you and I would like so much to pass on this magical key to you, so that always and in all situations you would be aware of the beautiful and the joyful, so that you too would live in a joyful euphoria as though you were walking across a multi-colored meadow. I am certainly not thinking of foisting off on you some sort of asceticism or made-up joys. I don't begrudge you all the real joys of the senses that you might wish for yourself. In addition, I would only like to pass on to you my inexhaustible inner cheerfulness, so that I could be at peace about you and not worry, so that you could go through life wearing a cloak covered with stars, which would protect you against everything petty and trivial and everything that might cause alarm.

Oh, Sonyichka, I've lived through something sharply, terribly painful here. Into the courtyard where I take my walks there often come military supply wagons, filled with sacks or old army coats and shirts, often with bloodstains on them. . . . They're unloaded here [in the courtyard] and distributed to the prison cells, [where they are] patched or mended, then loaded up and turned over to the military again. Recently one of these wagons arrived with water buffaloes harnessed to it instead of horses. This was the first time I had seen these animals up close. They have a stronger, broader build than our cattle, with flat heads and horns that curve back flatly, the shape of the head being similar to that of our sheep, [and they're] completely black, with large, soft, black eyes. They come from Romania, the spoils of war. . . . The soldiers who serve as drivers of these supply wagons tell the story that it was a lot of trouble to catch these wild animals and even more difficult to put them to work as draft animals, because they were accustomed to their freedom. They had to be beaten terribly before they grasped the concept that they had lost the war and that the motto now applying to them was 'woe unto the vanquished' [*vae vic-*

tis]. . . . There are said to be as many as a hundred of these animals in Breslau alone, and on top of that these creatures, who lived in the verdant fields of Romania, are given meager and wretched feed. They are ruthlessly exploited, forced to haul every possible kind of wagonload, and they quickly perish in the process.—And so, a few days ago, a wagon like this arrived at the courtyard [where I take my walks]. The load was piled so high that the buffaloes couldn't pull the wagon over the threshold at the entrance gate. The soldier accompanying the wagon, a brutal fellow, began flailing at the animals so fiercely with the blunt end of his whip handle that the attendant on duty indignantly took him to task, asking him: Had he no pity for the animals? 'No one has pity for us humans,' he answered with an evil smile, and started in again, beating them harder than ever. . . . The animals finally started to pull again and got over the hump, but one of them was bleeding. . . . Sonyichka, the hide of a buffalo is proverbial for its toughness and thickness, but this tough skin had been broken. During the unloading, all the animals stood there, quite still, exhausted, and the one that was bleeding kept staring into the empty space in front of him with an expression on his black face and in his soft, black eyes like an abused child. It was precisely the expression of a child that has been punished and doesn't know why or what for, doesn't know how to get away from this torment and raw violence. . . . I stood before it, and the beast looked at me; tears were running down my face—they were his tears. No one can flinch more painfully on behalf of a beloved brother than I flinched in my helplessness over this mute suffering. How far away, how irretrievably lost were the beautiful, free, tender-green fields of Romania! How differently the sun used to shine and the wind blow there, how different was the lovely song of the birds that could be heard there, or the melodious call of the herdsman. And here— this strange, ugly city, the gloomy stall, the nauseating, stale hay, mixed with rotten straw, and the strange, frightening humans—the beating, the blood running from the fresh wound. . . . Oh, my poor buffalo, my poor, beloved brother! We both stand here so powerless and mute, and are as one in our pain, impotence, and yearning.—All this time the prisoners had hurriedly busied themselves around the wagon, unloading the heavy sacks and dragging them off into the building; but the soldier stuck both hands in his trouser pockets, paced around the courtyard with long strides, and kept smiling and softly whistling some popular tune to himself. And the entire marvelous panorama of the war passed before my eyes.

Write soon. I embrace you, Sonyichka. Your R.

Sonyichka, dearest, in spite of everything be calm and cheerful. Life is like that, one must take it as it is, [and remain] brave, undaunted, and smiling—in spite of everything. Merry Christmas! . . .

R.

Bibliography

Arendt, Hannah. *The Origins of Totalitarianism*. New York: Schocken Books, 1951.

———. *The Human Condition*. Chicago: University of Chicago Press, 1958.

———. *On Revolution*. London: Penguin Books, 1963.

———. *Men in Dark Times*. New York: Harcourt Brace Jovanovich, 1968.

———. 'Civil Disobedience.' *New Yorker*, September 1970.

———. *The Life of the Mind*. New York: Harcourt Brace Jovanovich, 1978.

———. *Lectures on Kant's Political Philosophy*. Chicago: University of Chicago Press, 1982.

———. 'Philosophy and Politics: The Problem of Action and Thought after the French Revolution.' *Social Research* 57, no. 1 (Spring 1990).

———. *Ich will verstehen. Selbstauskünfte zu Leben und* Werk. Munich: Piper Verlag, 1996.

Blättler, Sidonia et al. 'Rosa Luxemburg and Hannah Arendt: Against the Destruction of Political Spheres of Freedom.' *Hypatia* 20, no. 2: Special Issue: Contemporary Feminist Philosophy in German (Spring 2005): 88–101.

Bloch, Ernst. *The Principle of Hope*. Translated by Neville Plaice, Stephen Plaice, and Paul Knight. Cambridge, Mass.: MIT Press, 1986. (Originally published as *Das Prinzip Hoffnung*. Frankfurt: Suhrkamp Verlag, 1959.)

Camus, Albert. *The Rebel*. Translated by Anthony Bower. London: Penguin Books, 2013. (Originally published as *L'Homme révolté*. Paris: Éditions Gallimard, 1951.)

Ettinger, Elzbieta. *Comrade and Lover: Letters to Leo Jogiches*. Cambridge, Mass.: MIT Press, 1997.

Evans, Kate. *Red Rosa*. London: Verso, 2015.

Frieling, Simone. *Rebellinnen. Hannah Arendt, Rosa Luxemburg & Simone Weil*. Berlin: Ebersbach & Simon, 2018.

Geras, Norman. *The Legacy of Rosa Luxemburg*. London: Verso, 2015.

Gordon, Jane Anna, and Drucilla Cornell, eds. *Creolizing Rosa Luxemburg*. London: Rowman & Littlefield, 2021.

Hermsen, Joke J. 'Who Is the Spectator? Hannah Arendt and Simone Weil on Thinking and Judging.' In Joke J. Hermsen and Dana Villa, eds., *The Judge & the Spectator: Hannah Arendt's Political Philosophy*. Louvain: Uitgeverij Peeters, 1999.

———. *Stil de tijd*. Amsterdam: Arbeiderspers, 2009.

———. *Kairos. Een nieuwe bevlogenheid*. Amsterdam: Arbeiderspers, 2014.

———. *Melancholie van de onrust*. Amsterdam: Arbeiderspers, 2017.

Hetmann, Frederik. *Rosa Luxemburg: Ein Leben für die Freiheit*. Frankfurt: Fischer, 1976.

Hirsch, Helmut. *Rosa Luxemburg: strijdbaar en menselijk*. Amsterdam: H. J. Paris, 1970.

Hoek, Cris van der. *Een bewuste paria. Hannah Arendt en de feministische filosofie*. Meppel: Boom, 2000.

Jacob, Mathilde. *Rosa Luxemburg: An Intimate Portrait*. Translated by Hans Fernbach. London: Lawrence & Wishart, 2000.

Kant, Immanuel. *Critique of Judgement*. Translated by James Creed Meredith. Oxford: Oxford University Press, 2007. (Originally published as *Kritik der Urteilskraft*. Berlin: Verlag Lagarde, 1790.)

Lleshi, Bleri. *De kracht van hoop*. Antwerp: Uitgeverij Epo, 2018.

Louis, Édouard. *The End of Eddy*. Translated by Michael Lucey. London: Harvill Secker, 2017. (Originally published as *En finir avec Eddy Bellegueule*. Paris: Éditions du Seuil, 2014.)

———. *Who Killed My Father*. Translated by Lorin Stein. London: Harvill Secker, 2019. (Originally published as *Qui a tué mon père*. Paris: Éditions du Seuil, 2018.)

Luxemburg, Rosa. *The Mass Strike, the Political Party and the Trade Unions* Translated by Patrick Lavin. Detroit: Marxist Educational Society of

Detroit, 1925. Available at: www.marxists.org. (Originally published as *Massenstreik, Partei und Gewerkschaften*, 1906.)

———. 'Rebuilding the International.' Available at: www.marxists.org. (Originally published as 'Der Wiederaufbau der Internationale.' *Die Internationale*, April 15, 1915.)

———. 'Order Prevails in Berlin.' Available at: www.marxists.org. (Originally published as 'Ordnung herrscht in Berlin.' *Die Rote Fahne*, January 14, 1919.)

———. *Brieven*. Dutch translation of Rosa Luxemburg's letters, introduction by Jacques de Kadt, translated by M. Verdaasdonk. Amsterdam: Van Oorschot, 1976.

———. *Gesammelte Werke*, Band I–IV. Berlin: Dietz Verlag, 1983.

———. *The Letters of Rosa Luxemburg*. Translated by George Shriver. London: Verso, 2011. (Based on the German selection of Rosa Luxemburg's letters *Herzlichst, Ihre Rosa*. Berlin: Dietz Verlag, 1990.)

Manin, Bernard. *The Principles of Representative Government*. Translated by J. A. Underwood. Cambridge: Cambridge University Press, 1997. (Originally published as *Principes du Gouvernement Représentatif*. Paris: Calmann-Lévy, 1995.)

Mills, Dana. *Critical Lives: Rosa Luxemburg*. London: Reaktion Books, 2020.

Nettl, Paul. *Rosa Luxemburg*. Oxford: Oxford University Press, 1966.

Nye, Andrea. *Philosophia: The Thought of Rosa Luxemburg, Hannah Arendt & Simone Weil*. London: Routledge, 1994.

Piketty, Thomas. *Capital in the Twenty-First Century*. Translated by Arthur Goldhammer. Cambridge, Mass.: Belknap Press of Harvard University Press, 2014. (Originally published as *Le Capital au XXIe siècle*. Paris: Éditions du Seuil, 2013.)

Reybrouck, David van. *Tegen de verkiezingen*. Amsterdam: Bezige Bij, 2016.

Roland Holst, Henriette. *Rosa Luxemburg*. Rotterdam: Brusse's Uitgeverij, 1935.

Rose, Jacqueline *Women in Dark Times*. London: Bloomsbury Publishing, 2014.

Schulman, Jason, ed. *Rosa Luxemburg: Her Life and Legacy*. New York: Palgrave Macmillan, 2013.

Solnit, Rebecca. *Hope in the Dark*. New York: Nation Books, 2004.

Tjeenk Willink, Herman. *Groter denken, kleiner doen*. Amsterdam: Prometheus, 2018.

Wimmer, Reiner. *Judische Philosophinnen: Rosa Luxemburg, Hannah Arendt & Simone Weil*. Tubingen: Attempta Verlag, 1995.

Zuboff, Shoshana. *Surveillance Capitalism*. London: Profile, 2019.

Acknowledgments

Writing an essay is an undertaking 'in concert' with others. While writing is a solitary activity, sharing the content and getting others to read it could in itself be called a political deed. I would like to thank Renée Borgonjen, Coen Simon, and Job Lisman for reading and commenting on earlier versions of this essay. My thanks also go to Cris van der Hoek and Brenda Ottjes, experts on the work of Hannah Arendt and Rosa Luxemburg, for their keen scrutiny; this allowed me to better stage the philosophical meeting between the two thinkers. I'm also grateful to my children, Rodante and Sebald van der Waal, for their critical comments, political perceptiveness, and youthful zest, giving me the necessary courage to finish this project, which was written particularly for their generation. I'm much obliged to all thirty members of the Rosa Luxemburg Reading Club for their enthusiasm and passionate discussions, as well as Stichting Amor Mundi and the International Institute of Social History in Amsterdam for kindly presenting this essay at a symposium in 2019. I would like to thank Jaap de Jonge for his love and support while I was writing this essay. Finally, my thanks go to Laura Vroomen and Singel Publishers for kindly permitting the use of part of Laura's translation of an excerpt from my book *Time on Our Side* in this book.

JOKE J. HERMSEN (1961) is a Dutch writer and philosopher, who studied in Paris and Amsterdam. She published *The Judge & the Spectator: Hannah Arendt's Political Philosophy* with Dana Villa in 1999. Her historical novel *De Liefde dus* (2004), about eighteenth-century philosopher Isabelle de Charrière, and her literary moral drama *Blindgangers* (2012) were nominated for the prestigious Dutch literary prize, the Libris Literatuur Prijs. Her essay on time, *Stil de tijd* (2010), was awarded the Jan Hanlo Essayprijs prize and has been reprinted many times. Both *Kairos: Een nieuwe bevlogenheid* (2014) and *Melancholie van de onrust* (2017) were nominated for best Dutch philosophical book of the year. Her most recent novel, *Rivieren keren nooit terug* (2018), is a story about time, memory, and a first love. *A Good and Dignified Life* is the translation of her most recent essay, *Het tij keren,* which has also been translated into Arabic, Spanish, German, Norwegian, and Danish.

BRENDAN MONAGHAN (1979) grew up in Botswana and read political science at the University of Amsterdam. After a spell at Amnesty International, he became a translator of history, politics, and philosophy from Dutch into English.